The Violence Continuum

The Violence Continuum

Creating a Safe School Climate

Elizabeth Cervini Manvell

ROWMAN & LITTLEFIELD PUBLISHERS, INC.
Lanham • Boulder • New York • Toronto • Plymouth, UK

Published by Rowman & Littlefield Publishers, Inc.
A wholly owned subsidary of The Rowman & Littlefield Publishing Group, Inc.
4501 Forbes Boulevard, Suite 200, Lanham, Maryland 20706
http://www.rowmanlittlefield.com

Estover Road, PlymouthPL6 7PY, United Kingdom

British Library Cataloguing in Publication Information Available

Library of Congress Cataloging-in-Publication Data

Manvell, Elizabeth C., 1951-
    The violence continuum : creating a safe school climate / Elizabeth Cervini Manvell.
        p. cm.
    Includes bibliographical references.
    ISBN 978-1-61048-566-1 (cloth : alk. paper) -- ISBN 978-1-61048-567-8 (pbk. : alk.
paper) -- ISBN 978-1-61048-568-5 (ebook)
    1. School violence--Prevention. 2. School environment. I. Title.
    LB3013.3.M274 2011
    371.7'82--dc23
                                    2011034793

∞™ The paper used in this publication meets the minimum requirements of American
National Standard for Information Sciences—Permanence of Paper for Printed Library
Materials, ANSI/NISO Z39.48-1992.

Printed in the United States of America

To everyone who cares about children and schools.

Contents

Acknowledgments   *ix*

Introduction: A Safe Haven   *xi*

Chapter 1   *Why Should Schools Teach Students to Be*   *1*
                  Smart and Good People?

Chapter 2   *How Are School Climate and Violence*   *13*
                  Prevention Linked?

Chapter 3   *What Do We Mean by Violence and Is It*   *29*
                  Really a Problem in Our School?

Chapter 4   *What about Issues of Diversity and Equal*   *41*
                  Protection Under the Law?

Chapter 5   *Is School Violence the Same for Everyone?*   *57*

Chapter 6   *What Are the Elements of a Safe School Climate?*   *77*

Chapter 7   *How Do We Intentionally Teach Our Children*   *99*
                  to Be Non-Violent?

Chapter 8   *What is the Role of School Staff?*   *111*

Chapter 9   *How Can Diverse Communities Work*   *123*
                  Together to Improve School Climate?

Chapter 10   *How Do We Take Our Vision and Make It Happen?*   *129*

Chapter 11   *How Do We Ensure the Changes Are Real*   *141*
                  and Lasting?

Glossary of Violence Terms   *147*

References   *149*

About the Author   *155*

Acknowledgments

Social justice and the responsibility to care for our children have long been driving forces in my life and career in education. Along the way, I have been lucky to meet people who share my vision and challenge me to think deeper. I have also benefited from all the students and parents I worked with who patiently taught me how to bring these principles to life in the classroom and school community. I would like to express my appreciation for some of those special people.

To my dear friend, Lillian Moss, I thank her for sharing with me her exceptional intellect and her continuous quest to be a better person and do her best for students. Lilly's wisdom lives in my head and now in the pages of this book.

To my soulmate, Allison Ewoldt, who has dedicated her life to making classrooms more challenging and child-centered, and the world a more life-affirming, sustainable place for future generations, I thank her for her enriching friendship. Allison never fails to inspire and energize me, and to help me know I am on the right track.

To my longtime teacher friends, Joan Koster, Sandy Moran, Ann Scalzo, and Pat Stacconi, I thank them for their encouragement when I was their principal, for their enthusiasm for trying new ideas in the classroom, and for our continuing lively discussions.

Writing a book is solitary work, so I especially appreciate the support I received from Kristina Mann at Rowman & Littlefield Education and from my family, including my parents.

The book is more cohesive and crisp thanks to the efforts of my daughter, Jessica Manvell, who volunteered to proofread the manuscript. She did so with an intensity and skill level I could only imagine and I thank her immensely. It was a wonderful mother-and-daughter bonding experience, one where we each learned a great deal about the other, including that we share the same vision for schools and for the world.

And as I usually do, I end my acknowledgments with a heartfelt thank you to my husband, Arthur Elfenbein, who continues his unwavering support of me and of my writing. He was especially interested in the topic of this book and was always anxious to explore new ideas with me. Arthur's insight and his own sense of social justice were added motivation to write a book that will touch many lives and make a difference.

Introduction

A Safe Haven

When the bully said out loud in class, "Why don't you go home and shoot yourself, no one will miss you," 17-year-old Eric Mohat did just that. He could no longer take the continuous harassment, and on March 27, 2007 he shot himself. His parents are suing the high school administrators and the classroom teacher who were informed of the bullying and saw it take place, but took no action. How is this the case when so much emphasis has been placed on violence prevention?

After the 1999 Columbine tragedy, we were challenged to ensure that our schools were safe—and to do it quickly. Parents, students, teachers, administrators, and communities demanded that schools take action. State legislatures enacted violence prevention laws and schools implemented crisis management plans and school safety policies and programs.

Yet, after more than a decade of targeted school safety efforts, violence in our schools is still a major issue, and discipline remains a concern for both teachers and parents. While deadly violent crime in schools has dropped, the incidences of bullying and harassment have not. The recently publicized deaths of middle, high school, and college students, harassed and hounded by other students to the point of suicide, has created a push to enact anti-bullying measures.

Children are suffering, many quietly. They skip school, become physically ill, drop out, and hurt themselves and others because we fail to acknowledge the pervasive, sometimes subtle, forms of violence that happen on our watch every single day. Children need—and we owe them—our help.

The antidote to school violence lies in a comprehensive safe school plan that builds a positive school climate. With such a focus, violence of all kinds is recognized and prohibited, and we take it seriously when students say they are being bullied. The support we provide and the efforts we make to teach and model positive social skills give our children a safe place to learn and grow to be good people.

What are the characteristics of an effective safe school climate plan? How do we ensure our efforts have a lasting impact?

A comprehensive safe school climate plan is intentional. It strives to create an emotional and physical safe haven where students can take the risks needed to learn. Intention is born in a thoughtful exploration of violence—in all its forms—and of how our written and unwritten policies, and the way we treat students, advance or thwart our chances of success. Half-hearted efforts to improve the climate of the school or leaving it to chance will not produce results. The power of intentional efforts to better the lives of our children and society is awe-inspiring.

A comprehensive safe school climate plan is introspective. Superficial efforts lead to superficial changes. Before we can move toward solutions, we need to define our personal beliefs and what we dream for our children, and then take an honest look at how we measure up. We need to understand violence is a continuum of acts—from subtle to overt—and that all violence taints the climate of a school. Introspection makes us evaluate the social-emotional and physical health of our school, and to see how we, as individuals, contribute to this climate. It creates ownership of the problems and of the solutions.

A comprehensive safe school climate plan is interpersonal. It is built on shared beliefs and a shared commitment. Members of our school community decide what is important to us, and why and how we should get involved. As a group, we explore the continuum of violence and define what we want our children and our school to be like. We make our vision a reality by sharing our collective goals with others in the classroom, the principal's office, our homes, and on the playing field.

A comprehensive safe school climate plan is internalized. We are motivated from within to care and to take action. We work together to steer our everyday interactions and our curricular, instructional, and classroom management decisions toward creating a positive school climate. This process builds a common belief system that profoundly changes both the school climate and school culture. School becomes a place where everyone takes violence prevention seriously. It becomes a safe place where we make good things happen.

A comprehensive safe school climate plan is inclusive. It recognizes that school does not feel the same to everyone. The way children feel depends on their personal experiences, how others view and treat them, and the nature of the relationships they have with the adults in the school. We make an effort to find out what is actually happening and how students and staff truly feel.

Our plan includes targeted prevention and intervention support for students who are bullied and harassed and those who bully and harass others, as well as for those who feel excluded or disconnected.

A comprehensive safe school climate plan is inexpensive. It recognizes that each school has a unique culture, circumstances, strengths, and challenges, and that while the desire to raise good children is universal, the path is not. Costly consultants and pre-packaged programs that have already identified the problems and provided the solutions bring changes that are cosmetic and temporary. We use a simple process to define what our particular school needs and then develop our own action plan to make it happen. Our thoughtful process brings about grassroots changes that are systemic and lasting.

A comprehensive safe school climate plan is idealistic and pragmatic. It is based on the ideal of a quality life, yet the plan is still doable. Through our planning we define a code of conduct, specify what is and is not tolerated, model what is expected, address all manifestations of violence, and prepare a crisis intervention plan. At the core, we have efficacy; we believe we can have a profound influence our children's behavior and attitudes. Then from pre-kindergarten to graduation, we systematically teach and expect them to choose nonviolent, respectful, and compassionate behavior.

Finally, a comprehensive safe school climate plan is inspirational. It makes us want to keep going. It helps people of diverse backgrounds and cultures find the common hopes and dreams we have for our children. It unites us behind a shared vision and becomes the foundation for everything that happens in our school. We celebrate the commitment and power we have to make our school and society healthier for everyone.

To create a comprehensive safe school climate plan we need to understand why it is important and necessary to do so. In chapter 1, we look at the role and obligation public schools have to teach and reinforce the human rights and responsibilities that are fundamental to a functioning society. We do this by developing students with a strong moral character who make intelligent, respectful, and constructive choices.

Chapter 2 explores how the climate and cultural norms of a school affect the type and prevalence of violence students face each day, and the impact this has on their ability to feel safe and learn. We hear what students say they want and need from us, and look at how well we are meeting their needs.

In chapter 3, we define violence as hurtful behaviors and an abuse of power used to intentionally hurt another person. We use the violence continuum activity to map specific acts of violence from the subtle to the obvious. By creating our own violence continuum, we uncover the range of emotional, social, and physical harm violence can do, and how these violent acts and attitudes affect our school climate and academic achievement.

With this understanding of what violence looks like and an acceptance of our obligation to provide students with a safe place to learn, chapters 4 and 5 focus on student diversity and how all children do not experience school in the same way. Students' experiences are affected by factors such as gender, race, ethnicity, socio-economic status, special learning needs, sexual identity, and the nature of their home life and the neighborhood in which they live. These chapters discuss ways to make our school climate one where those who are teased, excluded, bullied, and harassed are protected and supported.

In chapters 6 and 7, we learn about the four phases of a safe school climate plan that emphasizes prevention and early intervention. We learn specific ways to embed pro-social skills and respect for diversity in our classrooms in the curriculum materials and instructional practices we choose, and in our classroom management attitudes and methods.

Chapter 8 takes a close look at the critical role that teachers and principals play in setting the climate of the classroom and school. We look inward to examine how we view and treat our students, and identify and eliminate the things we knowingly and unknowingly do that hurt children.

Next, we move on to practical ways to generate interest among school staff and parents to improve the climate of our schools. Chapter 9 teaches us how to use essential questions to bring together a diverse group of individuals to define a common vision of the world we all want for our children.

The focus of chapter 10 is on the design and implementation of a safe school climate plan. We explore strategies and survey materials for gathering information about how our students, staff, and families feel about our school. Then we learn how to use this information to develop simple action plans that define goals, objectives, and initiatives that improve our school climate, and have a deep and lasting impact on school culture.

Chapter 11 ties together the concepts and information covered in the first ten chapters, and reminds us of our promise to ensure schools are a safe haven. It motivates us to continue our sincere efforts to embed — as a way of life — the ideals of empathy, respect, tolerance, and compassion in our schools and in the hearts and minds of our children.

Chapter 1

Why Should Schools Teach Students to Be Smart and Good People?

> The true test of civilization is not the census, nor the size of cities, nor the crops—no, but the kind of man the country turns out.
>
> —Ralph Waldo Emerson

What a wonder a school is—the orchestration it requires, the driving symmetry of purpose, the faith we have in others and their trust in us, the bonds that hold it together, and the promises it makes and the promises it keeps. A school is a unique sum of its parts—a powerful force for the common good yet committed to each individual. It is where we enlighten, refine, and elevate the quality and moral goodness of our children's civic, social, and private lives.

Nearly a century and a half after Emerson defined the true test of a civilization we are still concerned with the kind of men and women we turn out into the world. Character defines our personal lives and who we are as a society, and it is tested every day, in everything we do, in ways that matter deeply.

Where do we look for help with the formidable responsibility of *civilizing* our children so they make constructive choices that benefit themselves and their community? We have always relied on the family and religious institutions to nurture our children to be good people. Yet parents, communities, and our government also look to schools to fix our social ills. Amidst the clamor for highly skilled teachers, better test scores, and the stress of reduced funding, Americans believe that the primary purpose of a public school education is to "prepare children to become effective and responsible citizens" (Rose and Gallup 2000, 42).

Historically, schools have been seen as promising agents of social change and a great equalizing force for the common good. In this regard schools are a catalyst for changing thinking and improving the world. As human

1

understanding has evolved, so too have the expectations placed on the public education system. A PBS documentary that was aired in 2000 explored the purpose of public schools as seen over time. "School: The Story of American Public Education" identified civil rights, population growth, immigration, the rise of cities, and poverty as the major social and economic influences that shifted the focus of education. School violence was also included as one of the defining influences. The program concludes that public schools are expected to do many things besides teach academic content:

- Prepare children for citizenship.
- Cultivate a skilled workforce.
- Teach cultural literacy.
- Prepare students for college.
- Help students become critical thinkers.
- Help students compete in a global marketplace.

SCHOOLS ARE THE LOGICAL CHOICE

Schools—where children spend most of their waking hours—are the natural place to teach them to become responsible adults who show respect for each other on an individual, cultural, and human level. Attendance at school is something all American children have in common, the one sustained cultural experience they share. Horace Mann rightly called schools the "great equalizer" of the condition of humankind. For many, the secondary school years are the last time they will be part of an organized social group. This gives schools a tremendous opportunity, and a tremendous responsibility, to support the work of families and the needs of society by reinforcing moral behavior and principles of citizenship.

In his 1916 book *Democracy and Education,* John Dewey made a resounding impact on the public education system with his belief that the purpose of an education was not to just learn information, but to think about what we are being taught, experience it, and then apply what we learn to our life as a citizen in a democracy. His view that schools are the foundation of a just society implores us to create a climate for learning where students are expected to develop into socially responsible citizens and are given the tools to do so. He wisely cautioned that directing a child to change a physical behavior might result in compliance, but it does not provide the environment needed to develop a moral sense of right and wrong.

Children are not likely to learn strong ethics and peacemaking from the news or entertainment media, where violence is common and casual. Issues of character and ethics may never come up during a college education, and it is unlikely they will learn them in the business arena or from observing public leaders. It is our K–12 public schools that are expected to produce graduates who have a solid core of positive character traits and values to guide them successfully through work, college, personal relationships, parenting, and community life. Public educators have power, influence, and authority over what happens in our schools and classrooms. As a result we also have the power to teach our students to be good people.

55 million
Students enrolled in pre-kindergarten through 12th grade in United States in 2008.
(CDC 2008)

THE NEW GOLDEN RULE

Public schools are not overstepping their bounds when they teach values and character—it is inherent in our mission. The alternative would be schools as morally neutral institutions where no one took a stand about what was right and what was wrong. Not only would this be a tragic waste of a rich opportunity, it would be impossible to sustain. It would be chaos. Just the logistics alone of maintaining order and peace among hundreds and even thousands of students, diverse in many ways, requires clear expectations and guidance for behavior in a climate of common decency. And Americans do tell us that they believe schools should address students' behavioral, social, and emotional needs in addition to academics (Rose and Gallup 2007, 41).

By their design, schools always have and always will teach children how to be good and smart because both characteristics are critical components of a functioning school and civic life. Martin Luther King, Jr. believed in this dual purpose when he claimed, "The function of education is to teach one to think intensively and to think critically . . . Intelligence plus character—that is the goal of true education" (Character Above All n.d.).

Good character has long been simplified as *The Golden Rule*: "Do unto others as you would have them do unto you." This basic tenet of reciprocity— mutual care and concern—has been embraced by civilizations and religions for thousands of years. In ancient Greece, the saying was "Avoid doing what you would blame others for doing." In ancient Egypt, it was "That which you hate to be done to you do not do to another." Taoism says "Regard your neighbor's gain as your own gain, and your neighbor's loss as your own loss."

These different wordings all share a common vision of how human beings should treat each other. The message is this: If I do not like something, I will not do it to someone else. This is a good place to start. But for children to internalize the intended meaning of the concept, we must go beyond this egocentric application to the promise of mutual care and concern on multiple levels: that of the individual, one's culture, and all of humanity.

Each individual has a unique point of view, and there is the potential for conflict when people do not share the same likes and dislikes, perspectives and preferences. It is not enough to refrain from doing to another what *you* dislike. The other person is an individual with his own ideas of what is acceptable. If I like to be hugged and you do not, would it be okay for me to walk over and hug you? What if you like to take physical risks and I do not? Would it be okay for you to drive fast on mountain roads with me in the car? To treat each other with respect, we have to know and honor what the other person wants from us.

The same issue arises when considering different cultures. Cultures are based on specific customs, beliefs, ways of living, and expected and forbidden behaviors, which have a profound effect on who we are. With so many different norms there is always the potential for conflict among cultures. Again, it is not enough for us to treat others in ways that respect *our* culture. Cultures are specific in what they do and do not think is okay. If your culture expects women to cover their heads in public and mine does not, is it okay for you to force me to cover my head? What if your culture believes animals are sacred and my culture does not? Is it respectful and considerate for me to serve you meat for dinner? Not if we wish to show respect for the cultures of other people.

At a universal level all human beings have basic rights and needs that go beyond individual preferences or cultural norms. With this big picture view comes the understanding that each of us has unalienable moral and legal human rights that must be respected. This includes our right to life, dignity, free thought and speech, and freedom from emotional and physical harm, as well as the right to choose how to live and pursue our dreams. I cannot take your life, demean your worth as a person, silence your voice, or hurt you physically or mentally. It is morally and legally wrong to do so. We must respect and honor the basic human rights of each person.

We now see how the Golden Rule is, in fact, based on mutual concern and care that applies to individual preferences, cultural expectations, and basic human rights. This broadened understanding requires that we have the ability to put ourselves in someone else's place to see life through their eyes and know what is right for them. Through an exploration of the concept of reciprocity we go beyond parroting an axiom to having true appreciation for the most fundamental and virtuous of character traits: empathy. And empathy leads to respectful and compassionate conduct toward others.

This New Golden Rule of Empathy gives us fundamental principles to live by:

- I would not like you to ignore my personal wishes and feelings, so I will honor your personal wishes and feelings and expect you to honor mine.
- My culture may have different beliefs and customs from yours, so I will respect your culture and expect you to respect mine.
- Regardless of my individual perspectives and preferences or the norms of my culture, all people have basic human rights, and I will honor these rights and expect others to do so for me.

The climate of a safe school is founded on this empathy and mutual respect, and just as we set the climate in our homes, we control the climate in our schools. This realization is both profound and empowering. School and home should and can be places where children, the most vulnerable and needy among us, feel they belong and are protected. By design and dedication we can make schools a safe place for our children to live and learn, where no form of violence—including both overt acts and subtle discrimination—is tolerated by anyone, toward anyone.

MAKING LIFE CONNECTIONS

A critical element of a positive and safe school climate is a thought-provoking, personally relevant curriculum that provides real-life opportunities for students to apply what they learn. The connections students make with the content motivate them to learn more and in the process they clarify who they are and what they believe. Effective instruction teaches positive social skills at the same time as it teaches academics through quality learning experiences, student collaboration, and respectful exploration of differing perspectives. It encourages children to think critically, to have a voice, and practice positive life skills free from the threat of intolerance, ridicule, or harassment. A caring school climate and healthy culture reinforce the rights and responsibilities fundamental to a functioning society, and eventually lead to good citizens who . . .

- Work toward the betterment of the community, as well as for themselves.
- Are intrinsically motivated.
- Are guided by a sense of right and wrong.
- Are knowledgeable, critical and creative problem-solvers who make healthy decisions.

- Are empathetic and compassionate in their attitudes and treatment of others.
- Accept responsibility for their choices and believe in the importance of fixing the messes they make.
- Have a language of cooperation and conflict resolution that lets them express and make their needs known, without resorting to violence.
- Believe they have something to contribute to the world and the power to make it happen.

Though we recognize that by nature schools have a powerful positive influence on children, this list of characteristics still seems like a tall order. Public schools operate in a fishbowl of expectations and scrutiny, and they are inundated with changing and often restrictive academic requirements and teacher accountability policies designed to ensure that students do well on assessments. Under the umbrella of school improvement and high-stakes testing we are presented with new models for instruction and new programs to implement. With a narrow emphasis on standardized assessments we are forced to return to this aged paradigm of public school teaching: If I present it to you (and you pay attention), you will learn it (if you try), and then you should be able to prove you know it on a test (if you study).

The hyper-emphasis on academics based on knowledge and skills as both the means and the end assigns little value to developing the social-emotional side of our students where character is born. This failure conflicts with the public's broad expectations of our educational system and neglects to acknowledge that academic learning and character development provide a foundation for one another and cannot develop separately.

How do we meet the implied and expected (and usually unfunded) mandate to create and sustain a positive school climate that produces good people, while at the same time have students reach a high level of academic proficiency? It does not happen by chance. It takes awareness and dedication, a vision and some creative thinking.

76%
Americans who say they have trust and confidence in public school teachers.
Poll by Bushaw and Lopez (2010)

ACCEPT WHAT IS AND MOVE FORWARD

Not every child enters kindergarten knowing the alphabet, just as they do not all begin school with the self-discipline and social skills to work as part of a group or sit still and listen to a story. However, children really do want to learn, do well, and be productive members of a group, even if they are not sure how to go about it. It is our job to welcome them regardless of what they do and do not know. Teachers work diligently to choose quality academic materials and instructional methods to teach all children to read, write, compute, and think critically because we know that teaching academics goes far beyond waiting for a teachable moment to arise. It requires that we assess where children are and pick up their education from there. We know *how well* we are doing through continuous evaluation of student progress. This takes intent and self-evaluation, and when necessary a willingness to change *what* we are doing.

Problems arise when outside forces fail to realize it takes the same intensity of commitment to teach children to be responsible decision makers and peaceful problem solvers as it does to teach them academics. It is a plea you hear from teachers if you listen carefully. They do not decry their obligation to educate all children to high academic standards. What they do decry is that the push to a standardized test version of academic excellence has obscured the view of the child as a whole person: a developing, complex human being with unique talents and needs, and a spirit that deserves nurturing. Character might not be part of any formal standardized achievement test, yet it is the most important test of all, for intelligence without a moral framework is insufficient and even dangerous.

Teaching other people's children is a privilege. It is a huge leap of faith for parents to trust that we have their children's best interests at heart and will act *in loco parentis* — in the place of parents — with all the love and concern this implies. We promise and parents expect us to treat their children as individuals paying attention to who they are as a person, in addition to how they do as a student. Teachers see the link between a positive school climate and behavior and learning. We recognize that the basic obligation of a public education is to keep our students safe from harm of all kinds — emotional, psychological, and physical — while they are in our care, so they can learn and grow unhindered.

In one important way, students exist in a unique context similar to the military or prison: they are a captive audience. States mandate that all children of a certain age attend school no matter how uplifting or upsetting it is to them, whether they want to be there or not. It is important to be mindful of this concept of the captive audience, the reality that children cannot run from the hurtful behaviors found in school life, those that have a negative effect on their learning and emotional health. Parents do not have much choice but to turn their children over to us and trust we will protect them from harm. Children do not have much choice but to come to school and trust that we adults will take good care of them.

School can be a blessing or a curse depending on the climate and culture in which students find themselves. Children need to be in a state of emotional balance to attend and learn. They lose out on the educational opportunities they deserve if they are distracted by the fear created by an unsettling climate of violence. We might not have experienced a major violent incident at our school but some level of violence does exist. Accepting this fact clarifies our duty to ensure school is a place where children want to be, by creating a climate conducive to the growth of each child as a whole person, and by expecting and teaching children to choose nonviolent, healthy ways to communicate their needs and cope with life's stresses. For every child to feel safe and free to learn, both students and adults need to promise to be good people who show empathy, compassion, and respect toward each other. We all need to be guided by the New Golden Rule of Empathy. Such a commitment builds enriching relationships and reduces the chances that students will be hurt or act in hurtful ways. This provides the makings of a safe school climate.

Teaching our children to be good people cannot be accomplished by saying it to them once, nor can we find it in a pre-packaged program of activities, worksheets, and posters. It takes a personal and organizational commitment and sustained effort. Developing the ability to make good choices evolves over time and requires patient, caring, attention and modeling, just as does the ability to read or add and subtract. It can be learned naturally through the intentional guidance and modeling of teachers children respect.

As we acknowledged earlier, children vary in their level of development not only in the skills and knowledge they exhibit, but also in their moral and ethical understandings and behavior. Recognizing this reality, public schools must accept them graciously where they are and target efforts to help them grow. We must believe that each child has the capacity to be a good person if we are to give each child a fair chance to be successful. Teachers do this all the time with academics, building from where a child is with a belief that growth is possible and that goals can be set and achieved. We must also be proactive to prevent or change violent attitudes and behavior, and that means *teaching*, not just *expecting*, students to know and do better. Teaching is a naturally evolving developmental progression if we are in tune with our students, where they are coming from, and what we want them to achieve.

THE NEED TO DO SOMETHING

Our own experiences and statistics and headlines about risky behavior and escalating youth violence call out for us to do *something,* while at the same time the perceived enormity of student behavioral issues can overwhelm us. The pressure to implement comprehensive safe school plans that include codes of conduct, crisis prevention and management procedures, character education and civility instruction, conflict resolution skills, bullying prevention and respect for diversity come from the same sources that push academic achievement. The federal government, state legislatures and education departments, school districts, parents, the community, and even our national pride call for attention to this matter. Pressure also comes from our own desire to nurture and guide children to realize their potential, a desire which called us to become teachers in the first place. We accept this mandate to teach social, emotional, *and* intellectual competence and, as we are learning here, these goals are in no way conflicting.

Schools have always sought to instill the basics of a strong and ethical character along with the three Rs, but it now seems like a more difficult challenge.

628,200
Students ages 12–18 who were victims of
violent crime at school in 2005.
(CDC Study 2008)

One difference is a pervasive thread of violence and disrespect in our society that is disseminated through many forms of media. Popular culture does not always celebrate moral and ethical behavior and the benefits of cooperation and collaboration to resolve conflicts. Unfortunately, there are plenty of poor role models for children to imitate.

In addition, families are not as reverent of schools as they once were and are more apt to challenge our authority. We also expect *every* child to attend high school and graduate, whereas in the past the system removed weaker performing and misbehaving students and children with disabilities. We now have higher expectations for everyone and are under pressure to be more competitive in the global market.

Real life and the classroom offer contrasting environments for learning. Real life is subjective and expansive, open-ended and unpredictable, learner directed, and also allows children to develop at their own pace. Schools are predictable, traditionally teacher directed with predetermined content and objectives, and focused on specific performance indicators for each grade level rather than on a child's developmental level. We have made strides in connecting the two realities through creative instructional approaches, conceptually rich learning standards, motivating learning activities, and assessments that ask students to apply knowledge and conceptual understandings to problem solve real life situations. However, this is the aspect of education most threatened by the focus on test scores.

Proof of our commitment to the dual purpose of public education is the fact that in a climate of strong pressure from multiple sources to create academic

90%
Teachers surveyed who felt it was their job to intervene when they witnessed bullying.
NEA Study by Bradshaw et al. (2010)

results, many teachers are already *intentionally* trying to raise children who filter information and choose their behavior through a pro-social belief system. More and more we seem to agree that moral character, decision-making, and healthy life skills should not be learned by chance in school hallways or on the streets.

A CLIMATE THAT FOSTERS LEARNING

There is another reason to teach children and teachers to be good to each other. It is the concept of school as a *safe haven*. Learning is all about taking risks and trying the unknown, through modeling and trial and error. Students need a safe and secure learning environment to take these risks. When they step on the bus and enter the school they should be able to count on being valued for who they are and to know they will be cared for. They should expect to be treated well and to should know, in turn, that they are expected to treat others the same way. Our hearts and what we know about the human brain tell us that children cannot concentrate and learn if they do not feel physically and emotionally safe. For it to be a place to learn, school must be a safe haven, a sanctuary.

6%
High school students who reported they did not go to school one or more days in the past month because they feared for their safety. CDC Study (2008)

With a sense of belonging and security grows the courage to take emotional, psychological, social, and intellectual risks, and to rally from the inevitable setbacks. In such a climate, children learn they are capable and have power, and develop the confidence that they have something important to contribute, all under the principles of the New Golden Rule of Empathy.

It really is quite simple. We create the learning climate and we have the ability to change it if it is not a healthy one. This is the real foundation for learning and where our journey to develop smart *and* good children begins. We realize schools are a reflection of society, but we also believe schools are powerful agents of change that can elevate society.

Equations That Add Up
Good kids + Smart students = Responsible citizens

Chapter 2

How Are School Climate and Violence Prevention Linked?

You can't force commitment, what you can do . . . You nudge a little here, inspire a little there, and provide a role model. Your primary influence is the environment you create.

—Peter Senge

School is a place where you are not expected to already know, but where you are instead nurtured into knowing. Each school is an individual creation—a place with its own culture and climate that are the manifestation of the beliefs, attitudes, and behavior of the adults and children in the school.

School culture is the foundation of collective beliefs, attitudes, norms, standards, policies, and habits that drive what happens in a school. It is the operational blueprint and the origin of school climate. The culture of a school is like the culture of any group, community, or institution: a collective personality that can be identified by what members believe in and do as part of daily living.

School climate is the things that happen every day and the reaction people have to those things. These reactions stem from the school culture, which defines what is and is not expected, encouraged, and ignored, as well as who has power, and how they use it. The climate is how we are treated from our point of view. A positive school climate comes from *feeling* connected, powerful, valued, and safe.

School climate is
    how being in the school *feels*
        to each student and adult, and
            is specific to each school building
                and each classroom.

13

What do culture and climate look like in a school, and how are they related? They demonstrate the cause and effect relationship of a behavior (culture) and a reaction to how the behavior feels (climate).

Culture: A middle school offers free breakfast to qualifying students.
Climate: Students feel embarrassed to be singled out as poor, so they do not participate.
Culture: Teachers ask parents to contact them if there is a problem.
Climate: Parents feel intimidated by teachers and are afraid they will hear bad things about their children.
Culture: The school district transports elementary and middle school students on separate buses.
Climate: The younger students feel safer on the bus.
Culture: The school has a student-of-the-month program for each classroom with the award winners selected by their teachers.
Climate: The children not chosen feel bad and question why they weren't good enough to be selected.
Culture: Parent-teacher conferences are scheduled in the evening to accommodate working parents.
Climate: Parents feel the school recognizes the realities of family life and that teachers sincerely want to meet with them.

CLIMATE IS FLUID ~ CULTURE IS ENTRENCHED

WHAT DOES IT FEEL LIKE?

Every building, room, and natural space has a climate, and how we feel in that climate is the truth for each of us. Our reaction is personal, a product of our prior and current experiences, and our expectations. School climate reflects the relationships among members and how a child feels at school because of these relationships. What happens to children in the confines of the school affects how they feel, behave, and learn.

A positive school climate is a requirement for meeting the weighty goals of our public education system. It is the foundation of support for all that happens there. The emotional and physical climate of each school shows in the way students and staff treat each other. With mutually respectful relationships comes a peaceful, positive climate that supports academic achievement and social-emotional health. Unhealthy relationships damage the climate and create a culture of disrespect and violence where children cannot learn to their fullest.

School climate is sensitive. Our feelings and beliefs about school change as we have new experiences—both positive and negative. Perception *is* reality and in large groups such as in schools it is not easy to identify how each member feels. It is much easier to do this in small groups like families and close friends, and to respond by making adjustments to accommodate individual needs. In a family you know what each member likes and dislikes.

When children walk through the school door they assume the role of a *student* in a subculture that is school specific and complicated. The school has an overall feeling yet the climate can feel different to different students. How does the school feel—safe and welcoming or stressful and unfriendly? We cannot actually say because it does not feel the same to everyone. How the climate feels to an individual is not the same as the general climate. It is more specific and depends on a whole host of personal factors.

29%
6th–12th grade students who said
they had a caring school climate.
Search Institute Study, How Many
Youth Experience Each Asset? (2002)

A school shooting or student suicide reminds us of the importance of climate. We are shocked and want to know how such a thing could happen in a school of all places. We wonder how could a child be so lost. Talking to students helps us understand the realities of school from their perspective. They might tell us that if you are perceived as different in any large or small way, you are a target for exclusion and bullying. The group in power has a different perception of the school than the child who is unsure or alone.

Singling out the weak or outnumbered is a historically sad and dark side of human behavior that is especially upsetting when it happens in a school. Maryland State Superintendent of Schools, Nancy Grasmick (2006) evaluated the data on bullying in her state and shared these insights into who bullies, who is bullied, why they bully, and where they bully:

Who bullies?
• Most incidents are perpetrated by 13-year-olds.

Who is bullied?
• 12-year-olds are the most frequent victims of bullying incidents.

Why do students bully others?
- Motivation not known—21.2 percent
- Just to be mean—33.2 percent
- To impress others—21.2 percent
- Physical appearance—9 percent

Where does the bullying occur?
- On school property—84.7 percent.
- On school buses—13.3 percent.

Such victimization fuels outbursts of retaliation against others or violence toward our own selves. It shatters the belief that schools are safe havens. The reverence students and society may have had for schools as an institution to be trusted fades as the expectation of physical and emotional safety is reduced from a promise to a mere hope.

The primary question about school climate is whether our school feels safe and welcoming to *all* students and staff. If it does not, we are primed for lower academic achievement, lack of productivity, and escalating conflicts that result in disorder, sometimes to the point of emotional trauma and deadly violence. The good news is that we *can* make changes that improve the climate for all students. Since climate is how the culture of the school plays out, when we assess and mend school climate it makes us take a serious look at the deeply rooted culture of our school. Culture tells us what is okay and not okay according to the norms that are particular to that school. These cultural messages are conveyed formally and informally through written and unwritten policies, conscious and unconscious behaviors, and often endure for generations unquestioned. When we make that decision to candidly assess what we are doing, both intentionally and unintentionally, to the dignity and feelings of well being of each child and adult, we are looking at both climate and culture.

10%
Teachers in city schools reported being threatened with injury during the 2006–07 school year compared to 6% for rural schools.
NCES Study by Robers, et al. (2010)

POWER VERSUS DOMINATION

A healthy climate that is concerned about every member of the community is not static. Relationships change and need to be cared for and tended to regularly. Open, respectful communication makes sure we do not take our relationships for granted. Waiting for evidence that something is seriously wrong is passive and ineffectual, and comes with potentially dire consequences.

A secure learning foundation is cultivated and preserved by attitudes and actions that prevent problems from happening in the first place. This requires focusing our efforts on the prevention and early intervention levels of school safety. Violence prevention and early intervention reduce the chances that problems are left unresolved and allowed to escalate into a crisis.

Violence comes in many forms on a continuum from subtle to overt, and it has an amazing capacity to fester and grow. Violence is defined as physical force employed to violate, damage, or abuse another person, and as an abusive or unjust use of power. Think about the second part of that definition: violence is more than physical force, it is also something much more subtle— the use of power. This adds a new dimension to what we typically think of as violence.

Behavior, positive and negative, peaceful and violent, is an attempt to meet one or more of what William Glasser has identified as our five basic needs: belonging, freedom, fun, power and survival. For those lacking self-control and social skills, violence is often used as the way to force the fulfillment of one or more of these needs.

A safe school climate is built on the concept of power and efficacy, rather than the concept of dominance. Power is the ability to act to have needs met and efficacy is the belief that you have that power, the skills, and the resources to make it happen. It also infers that we have influence and are in control of our lives. When we are denied our basic need for power, fear, frustration, anger, depression and surrender set in. We either give up or fight back even harder. This is especially true of children and young people who are still dependent on adults. Without the social skills and personal resources and supports children need, violence can become the driving and disruptive force to gain or regain their power.

While power is a basic human need, one that helps us get our other needs met, dominance is a way people usurp or deny another person's power. To say someone is power hungry or is grabbing power implies the person is taking the power from someone else through domination. Children lose their power through life circumstances and to bullies and adults who take it.

People who have positional power such as parents, teachers, police officers, bosses, and legislators have the authority and responsibility to make decisions and step in if their organization is failing in some way. They are the keepers of the peace and the source of direction. The authority that comes with positional power is not permission to dominate, abuse, or break the spirit. Abraham Lincoln said, "Nearly all men can stand adversity, but if you want to test a man's character, give him power."

In healthy relationships people share power, even though some may have more authority than others. This is the basis of a positive school climate where everyone's needs are met. Sharing power can occur by participating in conflict resolution, through making decisions in class meetings, positive discipline approaches, and through learning activities that involve students personally. These processes give students a voice, a say in what happens and a respect for themselves and others. Sharing power gives students responsibility since they no longer rely on others to impose answers on them. Giving students the opportunity to exert personal influence builds their sense of efficacy as it teaches them to be thoughtful, empathetic, intelligent, and informed decision-makers, and exactly the engaged, tolerant citizens a democratic society expects from us.

76%
Parents of students in grades K–12 who feel their children are safe at school.
Gallup Poll by Carroll (2007)

A LEGAL AND MORAL DUTY

If 76 percent of parents think their children are safe at school, this means one in every four parents believes their children are in danger. A 2010 Phi Delta Kappa/Gallup Poll of the Public's Attitudes Toward Public Schools asked Americans what they considered to be the biggest problem their community's public schools faced. Lack of discipline was second only to school funding issues. Discipline sits at the top of teachers' lists of concerns as well. It is considered one of those unpleasant facts of a teacher's life, and in many cases contributes to new teachers leaving the field after only a few years. The loss of power felt when staring at a sea of students you do not think you can manage is very disconcerting.

Children are not violent and disrespectful in school purely because of the outside influences of popular culture, crime-ridden neighborhoods, misogynistic music, or poor family functioning. Violence creeps into our schools and thrives there because we let it. When we ignore and even condone harmful behaviors and attitudes we create a toxic environment.

A school culture that tacitly allows violence leads to students who feel anxious and fearful, and to absenteeism, poor academic performance, and more violence. Violence feeds upon itself; when we witness it or are a victim of it we are more likely to treat others badly. We grow to think this is what we need to do to survive. Tension builds when we are afraid of what might happen, and this tension puts us on edge and causes us to react strongly to a threat—perceived or real—by lashing out or withdrawing. For example, tension can come from a teacher worrying about classroom management or a child worrying if he will be bullied again today. The piling up of fears and protective behaviors erodes relationships. It robs us of our sense of security and results in an increasing undercurrent of violence. This is far from an ideal learning environment.

The connection between school climate and violence has received more attention in the past two decades, and is now understood to be a missing piece of the academic puzzle. Positive climate is recognized as the key to safe schools by 45 of the 50 state legislatures, the National Center for Disease Control, the National Parent Teachers Association, the National Education Association, child development and professional education organizations, colleges and universities, concerned citizens, and individual districts and schools through law, policy, and advocacy. There is agreement that we have a legal and moral duty to do better than we are currently doing, especially since our primary responsibility is to keep students safe. In 2011 New Jersey stepped up to enact the toughest anti-bullying legislation in the country, legislation where school climate was singled out as a critical factor schools must address.

Student Voices is a five-year study conducted by the New York State Center for Safe Schools that sought students' ideas on "improving learning, school safety, risk-prevention, and relationships." Researchers evaluated over 11,000 responses from middle and high school students in the state. When asked, "What can schools do to make you feel safer?" 52 percent of the students identified the need for improved "social dynamics, communication skills and responses." They felt metal detectors had little impact and "students sometimes see them as a challenge to be beaten." There was a consensus that the connection between the student and teacher is a critical component of student learning; over half of the students hoped to see a variety of and more innovative teaching using student-centered approaches rather than lecturing. Students tell us they want teachers who care about them and learning experiences that are engaging and relevant to their lives (Jalloh 2004).

55%
Students who said schools needed to increase teachers' trustworthiness to improve student-teacher relationships.
Five-year study by Jalloh (2004)

THE PROMISE OF A SAFE PLACE

If we take a close look at what goes on in schools we might wonder if the law of the classroom is the survival of the fittest. The National Center for Educational Statistics reported that in 2009 nearly 30 percent of students 12–18 years old reported being bullied in school. In a classroom of thirty students this translates into nine victims of bullying. In 2001 the percentage was 14 percent. While school killings, found at the overt end of the violence continuum, have decreased from the level of the first few years surrounding the turn of the 21st century, the behaviors we label as *bullying* have not.

Bullying is not an attempt to settle a disagreement. It is not a visceral reaction to a threat or conflict. Marlene Snyder is director of development of the Clemson University Olweus Bullying Prevention Project, a comprehensive, school-wide program designed for elementary, middle, or junior high schools. The program is designed to improve the social climate of classrooms, and reduce and prevent bullying and antisocial behaviors, such as vandalism and truancy. Ms Snyder is clear about the hurtful nature of bullying: "It's intentional, persistent, humiliating mistreatment between peers, dished out by those more powerful than their targets by virtue of size, age, numbers, money, race, or other characteristic. It's not a debate, argument or difference of opinion. It's an act of aggression intended to do harm" (Ollove 2010, 3).

The truth is many children are scared to come to school or ride the school bus. How can we in good conscience send our children to schools where they can be emotionally and physically hurt? Would we adults willingly go to a place that had a threatening climate? It is no wonder that children frequently dislike school and so many tune out and drop out. Arguing that bullying has always existed is not an excuse for doing nothing. Many educators are becoming more enlightened than to think it is merely part of growing up, a necessary evil that makes you tough and teaches you a hard lesson that you will use later in life. If anything, the lesson for life should be life affirming:

why it is not okay to bully or be bullied, what to do if it happens, and the importance of treating others with empathy and respect.

Denial that we have violence in our school and justifications such as those mentioned are indications that we may be out of touch with the reality of school life, or that we possess a limited view of what qualifies as "violence." Violence is real to the victim and children learn not to trust adults who deny it exists and fail to help them. Consider what this abuse of power must feel like to the victim; first is the power exercised by the bully and then there is that of the adults who deny the importance or even the existence of a problem. Denial damages children's belief in a caring world and shapes their world-view. When we break our promise to keep them safe while they are in our care, they are left looking after themselves with self-protections that often manifests as hyper-vigilance, avoidance, acting out, emotional and physical illness, and self-harm.

Interviewed by *Newsweek* magazine five years after the 1999 massacre that killed 15 and injured 24 in their high school, Columbine school counselors did not seem to understand how bullying escalates inequities in the way students are treated and creates an unsafe school climate. Four out of the five school counselors, who one would expect to be the most progressive and informed about issues of violence, said bullying was normal and natural, and they did not think bullying was much of a problem. One counselor said it was a *positive thing* ". . . to see kids beating up on other kids in our school, because it shows that things are back to normal" (Garbarino 2010).

29%
Students in 6th–12th grade who said they had the social competence to plan and make decisions. Search Institute Study, How Many Youth Experience Each Asset? (2002)

PROTECTIVE FACTORS

There is a growing body of evidence and resources that identify the "social learning" abilities needed to be a resilient nonviolent person. Ripple Effects, an organization that provides school climate information and survey instruments to schools, specifies seven key abilities that enable people to be successful in school, work, and relationships. And they advise that when some or many of these developmental assets are missing, we should take notice.

1. Empathy.
2. Assertiveness.
3. Impulse control.
4. Management of feelings.
5. Decision-making skills.
6. Self-understanding.
7. Connection to community. (Ripple Effects 1998–2007)

In "Early Warning-Timely Response: A Guide to Safe Schools" (2001) the U.S. Departments of Education and Justice also identify early warning signs of potential violence by children in schools. However they caution that behavior is contextual and specify how these warning signs should and should *not* be used.

1. Do no harm.
   "First and foremost, the intent should be to get help for a child early . . . not a checklist for formally identifying, mislabeling, or stereotyping children."

2. Understand violence and aggression within a context.
   "Violent and aggressive behavior as an expression of emotion may have many antecedent factors—factors that exist within the school, the home, and the larger social environment."

3. Avoid stereotypes.
   "It is important to be aware of false cues—including race, socio-economic status, cognitive or academic ability, or physical appearance."

4. View warning signs within a developmental context.
   "The point is to know what is developmentally typical behavior, so that behaviors are not misinterpreted."

5. Recognize the importance of multiple warning signs.
   "Research confirms that most children who are troubled and at risk for aggression exhibit more than one warning sign, *repeatedly*, and with *increasing intensity* over time."

With these cautions in mind, the early warning signs of a student's potential for violence identified by the U.S. Departments of Education and Justice include:

- Social withdrawal.
- Excessive feelings of isolation and being alone.

- Excessive feelings of rejection.
- Being a victim of violence.
- Feelings of being picked on and persecuted.
- Low school interest and poor academic performance.
- Expression of violence in writings and drawings.
- Uncontrolled anger.
- Patterns of impulsive and chronic hitting, intimidating, and bullying behaviors.
- History of discipline problems.
- Past history of violent and aggressive behavior.
- Intolerance for differences and prejudicial attitudes.
- Drug use and alcohol use.
- Affiliation with gangs.
- Inappropriate access to, possession of, and use of firearms.
- Serious threats of violence.

ARE WE WHO WE THINK WE ARE?

It is not only children who give signals when they are hurting and poised to lash out. Ripple Effects looks past the characteristics of high-risk *children* to characteristics of the climate in high-risk *schools*. A poorly functioning community affects students, parents, and anyone who works in the building. The warning signs refer to behaviors, attitudes, and social structures.

- There are obvious "in" and "out" groups.
- Name-calling is common.
- Charges of unfairness are not formally addressed.
- Rude or rough behavior is accepted.
- Discipline is inconsistent.
- Teachers feel afraid or under siege.
- Students feel disrespected by teachers.
- "Loners" are not recognized as being at risk.
- There is little or no public recognition for most students.
- School leadership is weak or disrespected. (Ripple Effects 1999–2009)

This list illustrates how a school is a complex system that creates an identifiable culture and climate, by which it is then defined. Cultures are powerful and their effects insidious; entrenched behaviors and attitudes, positive and negative, become the norm. Cultural "groupthink" sets in and responses become a habit:

If this happens, we do this. If that happens, we do that. Habits save us from the need to process mentally as we respond to the issues that arise each day.

These cultural norms make life less stressful and confusing and make us feel like we are part of something larger than our individual selves. Such culturally specific responses are pre-determined by tradition, policy, and expectations. Cultures can usurp individual power with behavior so automatic that we might do things we never thought we would do. But we reflexively stay within these norms where we are comfortable so we can remain part of the group, allowing us to meet our basic need to belong and to get along.

Read the list of questions below and think about the cultural norms in your school and classroom. Ask yourself: What do these norms say about what our culture believes about children and education? What do they teach children about self-discipline and responsibility? What do they tell students about power? How do they affect relationships between teachers and students, students and students, and teachers and parents? How do they influence the climate of the school or individual classroom? And lastly, do they reflect what we profess to believe?

Sample norms for behavior and discipline:

- How are rules and the code of conduct determined? How are they worded?
- What happens if a child breaks a class or school rule?
- What usually happens when a student is sent to the principal for discipline?
- What happens if two students get into a physical fight?
- What is done when a student verbally abuses a teacher?
- Are students allowed to send text messages or use cell phones during the school day?
- What is the procedure if a student tells a staff member that he is being picked on?
- How is name-calling and teasing handled?
- What happens when a teacher witnesses bullying or harassment?
- How do teachers work with parents when there is a problem?

Sample norms for classroom climate:

- When are children allowed to speak out loud and get out of their seats?
- What does the teacher do if a child is not paying attention?
- Is learning an active experience for students or do teachers address the class and lecture?
- How do elementary children line up and walk in the halls?
- What is the procedure for going to the bathroom? Getting a drink?
- How are students' desks or tables arranged? Do they choose where to sit?

- What happens when homework is not completed?
- How are partners or cooperative groups chosen?

Sample norms for accepting diversity and building community:

- Where are teachers positioned when students enter their classroom?
- What happens when a new child joins the class?
- What is done to prevent and address racial, ethnic, gender, and other slurs?
- How often does the entire school get together? For what purpose?
- When do students interact with the principal?
- How do students decide where to sit at lunchtime?
- How do upperclassmen treat freshman? How do eighth graders treat sixth graders?

Sample norms for power and what is valued:

- Which extracurricular activities are the most valued and get the most financial support?
- Are high school athletes disciplined the same as everyone else?
- Are the hallways, classrooms, bathrooms, and cafeteria free of litter and graffiti?
- How do parents participate in school life?
- How do teachers develop students' decision-making skills?
- Who interviews prospective teachers and principals, and what are they looking for?
- What is the teacher supervision and evaluation system? Do all new teachers receive tenure?
- How is appreciation shown for the efforts of students and teachers?

You can see how the culture as the foundation of the organization affects every relationship in the school community, every behavior, and every decision. It also becomes clear that the building principal, as the spiritual and instructional leader of the school, has the power to set the climate of the school, and the teacher has the power to set the climate in the classroom.

Individual teachers and principals might exercise their academic freedom to act against a prevailing cultural norm they feel is detrimental to students. This can create lone wolves or small groups of like-minded teachers within the school as a whole, or a create a principal who breaks new ground to do things differently. Classrooms are micro-cultures with micro-climates; students know in whose room they can be disruptive and whose they cannot, where they can laugh at other students and where they must be respectful, and which teachers value their relationships with students as much as the content they teach. Culture and climate change dramatically from one classroom to another because of the expectations and modeling of the individual teacher. Students feel different and have different expectations when they enter each room. They are quite astute at judging what is expected of them and responding to it in kind. They learn who we are by what we consistently say and do, and their behavior reflects this.

WHAT DO WE CHANGE?

If culture is the basis of what is done and climate is how this feels to those who experience it, then which is the easiest and most pressing aspect of school life to change? Is it the cultural norms as evidenced in beliefs, policies, procedures, and habits? Or is it the climate created by cultural attitudes and the imposition of cultural norms?

School climate is not only easier to change, it can do more in a short period of time to reduce violence, build relationships, and improve learning. Individuals and small groups *can* have immediate impact on the way the school feels to students and adults. We can change the way we treat students, discard undesirable practices, and replace them with desirable ones. When we stop and think about what we are doing, we are no longer products of the culture. Over time, these positive changes in climate influence the standard operating procedures of the school, and eventually the once entrenched culture evolves to reflect the changes in climate, and becomes healthier and more supportive of all students.

Consider the process of a neighborhood beautification project that is taking place in an area neglected for years. There is trash in the gutters, broken windows, and graffiti on fences and walls. At night the streets are dark and feel unsafe, and few venture outside. It has become a demoralized culture of not caring, isolation from others, and a sense of futility that anything can be done to improve the situation. There is little pride and sense of belonging. The cultural norms are to keep to yourself with your doors locked to isolate yourself from the disintegrating community that surrounds you.

But then a small group of residents decides to do something to fix up the neighborhood to make it look like a place where people care for and look out for each other. They pick up the trash from the gutters and plant flowers between the sidewalk and the street. They work with the police to remove the graffiti and ask city council to install brighter streetlights. They organize a neighborhood watch program and hold family-oriented block parties.

The word spreads. Others who live in the neighborhood notice the change in climate and start to feel like part of the community. They clean up their yards and paint flaking porches. They stop and talk with each other about the positive transformation and make new friends. They feel positive, safe, comfortable, and powerful.

The culture of the neighborhood begins to reflect the climate of pride that people feel. Over time the culture changes from one where it is okay to deface property to one where it is not, from one where you stay off the streets out of fear to one where you believe everyone has a right to enjoy the outdoors and the company of their neighbors. The observable changes in climate have led to a deeper change in culture with a new set of life-affirming norms to live by. The new overarching cultural norm is an expectation that neighbors care for each other and work to keep the community looking and feeling like a good place to live. It is a culture of positive action and collaboration, and a climate of pride and hope where members have a vested interest in the success of each person and in the neighborhood as a whole.

This change in climate altered how people thought about themselves. Their self-fulfilling prophecy became the belief that we can do anything to which we put our minds. If something like this can happen in a neighborhood it surely can happen in a school where members already have a common bond and spend hours of time together.

Schools go through a similar process when they realize how the climate and underlying culture of the school are affecting violence, character development, and academic achievement, and they decide to do something to improve students' experiences. They decide they want their school to be a thriving community where members look out for and protect each other, and where individuals, diverse in many ways, are welcomed and respected. Their attitudes and behavior change and take the school in a new direction.

Waiting for a violent tragedy as the impetus for such change is foolhardy and irresponsible. A tragedy can quickly and profoundly damage the climate of a school and have a long-term negative effect on school culture. It challenges our beliefs about who we are and our ability to make a positive difference. Once we understand how school climate, school culture, and school violence are related, we have no choice but to intentionally make our school the safe haven it is meant to be and that we have promised it will be.

Equations That Add Up
Power + Efficacy = Non-violent choices
Emotionally + Socially + Physically safe
= Positive climate

Chapter 3

What Do We Mean by Violence and Is It Really a Problem in Our School?

The greater the power, the more dangerous the abuse.

—Edmund Burke

Teachers are not detectives or crime scene investigators, paramedics or emergency room staff. In these jobs an emotional distance is necessary to survive work that involves one tragedy after another. In schools, where children are under our care, we can never allow ourselves to become desensitized to violence.

The staff of a school sees its fair share of heartbreaking, frustrating situations, yet the ethos of teaching could not be any further from that of emergency responders. As educators we tend to the whole child and are frequently their first line of defense. We work in the prevention department. To do our work successfully and fulfill our professional creed we must maintain our sensitivity and empathy for our students and their families, and continue to be incensed and take action at every assault on a child's dignity or person. We believe what happens to one of us happens to each of us and that we are all uplifted by respect and demeaned by violence.

The Center for Disease Control considers youth violence to be a public health issue, with school violence a serious subset of this category. Their "Understanding School Violence Fact Sheet" (2008) provides data on the extent of violence in American schools. This is what they found our children live with everyday:

- Approximately 30 percent of students report bullying happening in their school *sometimes* or *once a week or more.*

29

- A majority of the students reported being observers of the bullying, while 13 percent acted as a bully, 10.6 percent were bullied, and 6.3 percent were both bully and bullied.
- 31.5 percent high school students were in a physical fight during the previous year.
- 22.3 percent were offered, sold, or given illegal drugs on school property during the previous year.

These numbers are staggering when you take into consideration that the rest of the students are potential witnesses or accomplices to these behaviors.

THE POWER AND INTENT TO HURT

Statistics tell us violence does affect our children but also that schools are hardly the dens of *deadly* violence media accounts of school shootings would seem to indicate. Have the tragedies in recent decades created a skewed view of the life of a student? How do we know if we are overreacting or doing enough as we try to keep our schools safe?

The answer depends on what you believe falls under the heading "violence" and your understanding of how violence compounds and escalates over time. While overt acts of physical violence get most of the attention, the kind of violence that happens daily in our schools is on the more subtle range of the violence continuum. Affronts pile up and eventually explode if we do not notice early warning signs of violence. We have probably seen it in our own lives when we suffer in silence until we cannot stand it anymore. Our reaction comes out all at once—and not usually in the most constructive way.

< 2%
Homicides and suicides among 5–18 year-olds that occurred at school.
National Center for Educational Statistics (2009)

Violence exists on a continuum ranging from subtle, hurtful acts to those more noticeable and physically harmful. This broad view of violence is necessary when we are talking about schools where children have little or no power to remove themselves if they find the climate uncomfortable or threatening. Remember, they are a captive audience; they cannot get up and leave.

We have already defined violence as intentional physical force, emotional torment, and abuse of power, designed to intimidate, dominate, or inflict pain on another person. But without a common *functional* understanding of violence, any effort to make our school a safe place is already doomed. We can only correct what we recognize as a problem.

MAPPING THE VIOLENCE CONTINUUM

A continuum is a coherent whole characterized as a collection, sequence, or progression of characteristics or values varying by minute degrees. For example, the visible light spectrum moves along the continuum from red to orange to yellow, green, blue, and violet. Each element is similar to those on either side and there is a gradient of shades that transition one color to another. Yet the difference from one end of the continuum to the other is great.

Creating a continuum of behaviors is a simple and dramatic way to illustrate violence as an abuse of power and a desire to inflict emotional or physical harm on another. It gives us a graphic representation of the verbal and emotional abuse kids heap on each other and of more overt physical assaults. This is a unifying group activity in itself and a point of departure for future discussions about what we want for our children. It becomes the core of all our school climate and violence prevention thinking and efforts.

To create a map of the violence continuum gather a group. This group could be teachers at a faculty meeting, parents and teachers at a PTA meeting, a school climate team, or students in a classroom. Write the definition of violence on the board or chart paper and read it over with the group. Pass out a supply of small self-stick notes to each person and ask the participants to jot down as many forms of violence as they can think of, writing one per individual note. Participants can work alone, or together in pairs or small groups, as long as it does not interfere with an individual's flow of ideas. Participants should be reminded that it is a brainstorming session and that all ideas are respected and considered.

When time is up (five to ten minutes is usually sufficient), post a large sheet of paper and across the top write the heading, "The Violence Continuum." Draw a long arrow across the paper from left to right, and label the left starting point of the line segment "1 — Subtle" and the right end point "10 — Obvious." Mark the mid-point 5 (Figure 3.1). Paper, rather than a white or black board, provides a permanent artifact of the group experience and can be used in future discussions.

The Violence Continuum

Subtle 1   **5**   **10 Obvious**

Ask group members to come up to the drawing a few at a time to post their examples of violence where they think they best fit on the continuum. The chart they create is fluid and no two charts will look exactly the same. Participants may talk amongst themselves as they decide where to place the examples and may keep or change their placement after reconsidering some of the other examples being added. When they are done, everyone steps back and observes the results. In front of them is a continuum of behaviors meant to hurt others.

Give the participants time to reflect on what they see and what it tells them about violence. Ask if they agree with the placement of each example. Let them make justified suggestions for moving and grouping items and ask for group consensus. Out of respect for each member, ask the person who placed the example if it is okay to move it elsewhere on the continuum. Stack multiples together and add additional examples of violence that members think of during the discussion.

The discussion itself is the heart of the process, bringing members to a powerful level of introspection and evaluation. As they explore their own and others' beliefs and attitudes about violence and think about their own behavior, they come to understand the pervasiveness of violence, and the effect it has on the climate of their classrooms, schools, and homes. They experience the magic of a collective epiphany.

A pattern will likely emerge as the group discusses and organizes its ideas. Behaviors such as these will likely cluster at the "subtle" end of the continuum: ignoring, exclusion, rejection, teasing, whispering, name-calling, spreading rumors, and dirty looks. Overt acts such as fist fighting, stabbing, harassment, gay-bashing, hate crime, rape, suicide, and murder cluster at the "obvious" end of the continuum. Occupying the middle of the span are likely to be actions such as hitting, bumping, shoving, stealing, chasing, verbal threats, cyber bullying, unwanted sexual overtures, extortion, getting in someone's face, and taunting.

WHAT DOES THE CONTINUUM TELL US?

The violence continuum identifies physical, emotional, and indirect violence. It is based on overtness, rather than degrees of seriousness. It is important not to diminish the significance of the more subtle forms of violence—those low-key, emotionally damaging, insidious destroyers of relationships—which would only perpetuate the discounting of such behaviors.

Ask participants if, when they were in school, they experienced any of the types of violence on the continuum as a perpetrator, bystander, or victim. Give them an opportunity to share their personal memories, being sensitive to the courage it takes for a group member to share a particularly painful story of being a victim

60%
Violent incidents reported to Maryland State Department of Education from September 1, 2005, to January 31, 2006, that involved teasing, name-calling, and threatening remarks.
Report from Maryland Superintendent of Schools (Grasmick 2006)

or an admission of acting like a bully. To get the group to open up, share one or two of your own experiences. Connecting with the feelings they experienced and listening to the stories of others fosters empathy and compassion.

From here it is a short step to the realization that most, but not necessarily all, of the violence experienced in school lies in the subtle to middle range of the continuum. Yet where have schools spent their resources and put much of their efforts? We focus on the overt "crimes" and less so on the contributing causes leading up to the act. We take measures designed to prevent the less than two percent of the violent deaths of school-age children that occur in schools while overlooking the much larger number of children who are being bullied and harassed every day. Gun detectors, pat downs, video surveillance cameras, restricted entry, resource officers, clear backpacks, and security guards do not help to address this undercurrent of violence.

These measures, while helpful and necessary in some settings, can also create a false perception that a school is a violently hostile place. In the article "Overreacting to School Shootings Intensifies the Problem," Fox and Levin (2010) lament the faulty thinking that turns schools into "armed camps." They contend that drastic security measures raise the anxiety level of students by implying that violent students are everywhere, waiting to strike. It fosters the belief that violent retribution is a valid solution to being bullied.

Drastic security measures reinforce another faulty belief that violence consists only of physical harm. Discuss with the group the kinds of violent behavior they see on a daily basis in their schools, classrooms, and homes, and they will likely tell you what concerns them most are the pervasive verbal put downs and name-calling, exclusion, and lack of respect students direct at each other and at adults.

The plentiful examples at the subtle end of the continuum illustrate the mean-spirited isolation and demeaning of those who are perceived to be different or of lower status. This is based on jockeying for positions of power and influence, and all along the continuum we see how this feeling of power over another person is used to dominate. We know that power is a basic need and people do not give it up easily. But power *over* is not the same as power to make things happen.

This activity can dramatically change people's conception of school violence. While a murder, shooting spree, or suicide is newsworthy and devastating to individual lives and society's morale, statistically it is still an extremely rare occurrence in a school. Nonetheless, violence does happen regularly among students, and between students and staff, in *all* schools. The map of the continuum of violence we created highlights why we need to concentrate on the violence at the subtle end of the continuum, rather than worry about the infrequent deadly tragedies that make the news.

During the violence continuum mapping activity, the group might notice the potential for the escalation of behaviors along the continuum. Subtle acts of violence are emotionally and socially damaging by themselves and can escalate into the more obvious and physically harmful levels of violence, unless we use our influence to intervene early. Bullying and harassment might take on a more sinister intensity and progress to physical assaults, where it is not enough to upset the other person, he needs to be hurt physically as well. In a negative school climate, it takes students less time and provocation to reach the physically hurtful range of the continuum, where hateful slurs are hurled, threats made, and physical attacks occur.

Into school, a place we think of as a safe haven for our children, some have brought anti-social and destructive behaviors along with a hair trigger. Others have brought an underdeveloped sense of right and wrong and are easily influenced to do bad things. Thanks to the violence continuum, we now have a better understanding of how we can have an immediate, positive influence that will improve the safety of the school and the emotional climate. We now realize we can do this by intervening early and setting clear expectations for what *is* and *is not* okay. And the violence continuum tells us what to look for.

ACCEPTING RESPONSIBILITY AND LEADING THE WAY

The role of leadership in reducing school violence by improving school climate cannot be overstated. School violence prevention is a topic of concern at all levels of government, education, and society. This attention is valuable, yet the most important leadership comes at the point of implementation: within the building and the classroom. Principals and teachers are the true leaders, the ones who have direct and sustained contact with students every day. This contact provides a tremendous opportunity and responsibility to model, teach, and support peaceful pro-social behavior.

Thanks to a better understanding of what constitutes violence and how it can escalate, we now realize that no school is violence-free. We have to do something, even if well-meaning people around us say it's nothing to worry about, they'll outgrow it, everyone does it, it's part of the youth culture, and kids are just being kids. We have to be able and willing to look objectively at the children we love and teach and to recognize when they need help.

When two twelve-year-old middle school boys hogtied a younger student with pink duct tape and left him trying to get free in a deserted hall, the principal responded, "These two older kids generally do not cause any problems, and they more than likely were not truly intending to harm the student" (Houk 2011). This whitewashing comment shows a lack of understanding of what *hurting* another person means, that hurting can be physical, psychological, and social-emotional. We could make a list of all the planning and types of violence it takes to track down the targeted student, abduct him, hold him down physically and keep him quiet, tape his wrists together, tape his ankles together, then tape his wrists and ankles to each other behind his back. One of the fathers said, "Boys will be boys, but they've got to learn their limits." The message: A little bullying is okay.

0%
Difference between the number of public and private school students ages 12–18 who reported being bullied at school.
U.S. Department of Education Study (Neiman 2011)

Experts agree that we have a long way to go to educate children and adults about the boundaries of acceptable behavior. Dr. James Garbarino, author of many books on youth violence, frames it this way: "Bullying is not a rite of passage, it's not character-building, it's traumatic. And like any kind of trauma it needs to be understood and addressed" (2010).

Classroom teachers are best positioned to address the violence that hovers at the lower end of the continuum. They, especially elementary and middle school teachers, have the advantage of a more contained classroom community and regular access to a consistent group of students. Building on the relationships they have established with students, they can actively teach and model pro-social skills, see patterns as they emerge, and seek help for a student.

Anti-social behavior clustered in the middle of the violence continuum can be addressed in the classroom if the problem is brought to school professionals for advice and parents are immediately notified. In this case, everyone is committed to breaking the trajectory of escalating violence by finding out what is going on in the child's life and setting up needed supports and limits. Students, especially those who are or feel disconnected to others, need to be actively supported so they are not victimized or driven to use violence in retaliation.

The violence continuum helps us keep an eye out for the behavior that tells us a child is in crisis. The Center for Disease Control has identified the ways in which a bullied child may give us clues to his pain:

- Comes home with damaged or missing clothing or other belongings.
- Reports losing items such as books, electronics, clothing, or jewelry.
- Has unexplained injuries.
- Complains frequently of headaches, stomachaches, or feeling sick.
- Has trouble sleeping or has frequent bad dreams.
- Shows changes in eating habits.
- Hurts himself.
- Is very hungry after school from not eating lunch.
- Runs away from home.
- Loses interest in visiting or talking with friends.
- Is afraid of going to school or other activities with peers.
- Loses interest in schoolwork or begins to do poorly in school.
- Appears sad, moody, angry, anxious, or depressed when he comes home.
- Talks about suicide.
- Feels helpless.
- Often feels like he is not good enough.
- Blames himself for his problems.
- Suddenly has fewer friends.
- Avoids certain places.
- Acts differently than usual. (Hamburger 2011)

You may have noticed that most of these warning signs are avoidance or defensive behaviors rather than openly offensive attacks. These attempts to protect oneself are how children cope with the violence they are experiencing. We want children to *want* to come to school and they look to the adults in their lives to provide stability and limits, and to make school a great place to learn.

In a 2010 National Education Association study, 62 percent of teachers reported that they had witnessed bullying two or more times during the previous month. While 93 percent of school teachers and support personnel reported that their district had a bullying prevention policy, only 54 percent of the staff reported they had received any training (Bradshaw et al. 2010). We do not know the quality or intensity of training these individuals received or if it consisted of a one-time awareness meeting or memo. Limited or no training does not prepare teachers to recognize warning signs and to intervene early and properly. It also does not provide enough thoughtful engagement to establish a personal connection with the concepts behind the changes we are asking them to make.

School staff have an interest and desire to stop bullying, yet there is also despair and helplessness. Listen carefully to the conversation in the staff lounge and you may hear frustration and negative opinions about certain students who have behavior problems. You may also hear complaints about the lack of support from their families and school administrators. A teacher's feeling of efficacy that she has the power to make a difference can be eroded over time, just as a child's belief that adults will protect him can be eroded. Positive school climate efforts that are well-thought out and comprehensive can restore teachers' belief in themselves and their students' belief in them.

50%
Students committing homicide in a school who gave a warning signal about what they were going to do. CDC Report (2008)

A GLOSSARY OF VIOLENCE

What specific kinds of violence must we protect students from and what kinds of limits and interventions must we implement? This brief glossary of types of violence below, and the expanded glossary in the appendix, help us to understand the nuance of both the subtle and obvious hurtful behaviors that make students dread school.

Keep in mind that if committed outside of the context of school most of these actions would be considered a punishable criminal offense. Behavior labeled by the catchall term "bullying" when committed by young people becomes a crime when they become adults or the court decides to try them as adults. We should not excuse such acts by students who are developmentally mature enough to know better.

Glossary of Types of Violence

- Assault: an unlawful physical attack upon another; an attempt or offer to do violence to another, with or without battery, such as holding a bat in a threatening manner.
- Bashing: unprovoked physical assaults against members of a specified group such as gays and racial and ethnic minorities.
- Denigrate: to belittle someone, to treat them as if they lack value or importance.
- Embarrass: to cause confusion and shame and make uncomfortably self-conscious.
- Extort: to take money, information, etc. from a person by violence, intimidation, or abuse of authority such as force, torture, or threat.
- Glare: to stare at fiercely or angrily with a piercing look.
- Gossip: a conversation involving malicious talk or rumors about other people.
- Hate crime: a crime, usually violent, motivated by prejudice or intolerance toward a member of a gender, ethnic, racial, religious, or social group.
- Intimidate: to make timid and fill with fear.
- Misogyny: hatred, dislike, or mistrust of women.
- Sarcasm: a sharply ironical taunt or cutting remark.
- Sexual Harassment: persistent unwelcome directing of sexual remarks and looks, and unnecessary physical contact at a person.
- Tease: to irritate or provoke with persistent petty distractions or other annoyance, often as "fun."
- Taunt: to mock in a sarcastic, insulting, or jeering manner.

This is quite a list and it is only a sampling. Without the benefit of the violence continuum activity we would have only scratched the surface of what school life is like for our students and missed so many of these hurtful behaviors.

JUST A JOKE?

Sometimes a perpetrator claims a violent behavior was done to be funny (ex. teasing, sarcasm, putting a foot out to trip someone, posting an embarrassing picture on Facebook, libelous graffiti, practical jokes, grabbing someone's hat and not giving it back). She says that she was only kidding, or that she was misunderstood. These manipulative "excuses" do not mean the behavior was not offensive to the other person. We cannot always know a person's true motive and therefore are not always able to determine if the perpetrator's intent was really just to be "funny," or if it was to hurt someone under the guise of humor. We can, though, tell how funny the "joke" was by how the target reacts. Teasing and sarcasm often have enough of a basis in truth to be hurtful and embarrassing, regardless of intent.

This is when we need that new, broader understanding of the Golden Rule. To assess whether an act was innocent fun or covert violence ask the students involved some questions: Was the behavior unwanted? Did it interfere with the person's learning? Did it discriminate? Did it make the person feel: uncomfortable, nervous, afraid, embarrassed, humiliated? What would a reasonable person think if this happened to him? (The *reasonable person standard* is a legal test for determining harassment or a hostile environment.) If the answer is yes to any of these questions then the behavior is disrespectful and inappropriate and should be stopped.

There is a difference between humor and covert aggression, but with both the target is often accused of not having a sense of humor or of being too sensitive. How do *you* take teasing, practical jokes, and sarcasm? Put yourself in these situations. Have you ever been witness to someone being overpowered and thrown into a pool by someone stronger who thought it was funny? How about pinned down and tickled no matter how much you protested? Or teased about something you said or did that you thought was shared in confidence?

These manipulative behaviors put you off balance and that is the intention. They shift the balance of power in the perpetrator's favor. Teasing and sarcasm are sideways shots at your vulnerability, a way to get to you behind a false smile. Adults also find it difficult to be victims of these manipulative behaviors without being affected.

No matter how we look at it, the behaviors that span the violence continuum—from subtle to obvious—are insidious and unhealthy for everyone involved. They all hurt.

Equations That Add Up
Violence continuum + Intervention = Safer schools

Chapter 4

What About Issues of Diversity and Equal Protection Under the Law?

The highest result of education is tolerance.

—Helen Keller

Given all the press to the contrary, we are not as different from each other as we might think. People share many universal needs, traits, and behaviors that we call human nature. However, within that commonality of human nature each individual possess a unique combination of characteristics, temperament, beliefs, attitudes, and behaviors. With such individuality, friction and conflict arise. A lack of respect for these differences is a major source of violence, and we have a choice to exacerbate differences or to strive to understand them and focus on our commonalities. When we connect to basic human needs, we can transcend more superficial differences. A basic level of tolerance and a sincere desire to get along are necessary components of a peaceful community.

Violent acts motivated by ignorance, intolerance, and hate have an especially deep affect on the victim, and when they occur in a school they create a threatening climate for whole groups of people. No one in that "group" feels safe. They feel anxiety brought on by the fear that they might be the next target, a target for no reason other than a perceived difference by someone who does not even know them.

Growing up I was teased about my red hair. Someone would yell "carrot top" or "hey red" to me as they drove by. That was the extent of the teasing except for comments about the hot temper that was supposed to go with the red hair. I had an obvious physical characteristic for which I could be singled out. But I was spared the recent phenomenon of harassment of "gingers" who are attacked for no other reason than the color of their hair. A Facebook hate group announced that November 20, 2009 was "National Kick a Ginger Day." It made our local news when students at an area middle school participated. This was the first I learned of a historical prejudice in Great Britain against people with red hair. I imagined what it would be like to live in fear of random harassment for the way you look, by people who are strangers.

In previous chapters we discussed how schools have an unequivocal responsibility to protect the rights, safety, and dignity of all students. All disrespect hurts, and subtle affronts like name-calling and exclusion because of a group to which you belong create an environment in which prejudice is condoned.

Since diversity is a part of everyday American life, there is no way to sidestep the emotionally charged issue of intolerance in schools. Intolerance can be based on race, economic status, gender, sexual preference, disability, or some other classification, and it is a major cause of strife in students' lives. Intolerance is a driving force behind the violence continuum, as excluding, name-calling, and teasing escalate into humiliation and bullying, or on to harassment and physical assault.

Diversity training for adults is a critical part of any school climate plan focused on reducing animosity and violence between social groups. Teaching tolerance for differences is most successful when it is an integral and widely accepted tenet of the school climate, school culture, academic curriculum, and of prevention and early intervention efforts. A tenet is a central belief, not a separate program adopted to address a particular situation. It has depth and longevity.

77%
Elementary and middle schools who reported they participated in a program to prevent bullying.
CDC (2008)

WHO ARE WE?

The results are in and they paint a culturally rich and dynamic picture of who we are and how America continues to change. The 2010 U.S. population census documents what many of us have seen in our communities: our population is growing and it is more ethnically and racially diverse than ever before. We live in a society of cultures and subcultures that are rich with differences. The more we are exposed to, learn about, understand, and tolerate that which is different from us, the more harmonious a society we create. In the words of Albert Schweitzer, "The first step in the evolution of ethics is a sense of solidarity with other human beings." Schweitzer is speaking of empathy toward all, not just toward human beings who meet particular criteria.

Both in and out of school, children are surrounded by diversity, and they bring the beliefs of their parents, both healthy and unhealthy, to the classroom, to the bus, and to the athletic field. Students often zero in on their differences and use them to segregate into groups. And some then target other groups with violent, harassing behavior. All violence is a problem, but schools must be especially vigilant in preventing and responding to violence that crosses the line from bullying into harassment, discrimination, and hate-motivated violence. The federal civil rights laws that guarantee the rights of protected groups because of sex, race, religion, color, or national origin, age, and people with physical or mental disabilities serve as an extrinsic motivation for this due diligence. The Iowa Department of Education Anti-Bullying/Harassment Policy is especially comprehensive. It goes far beyond the federal laws to define seventeen protected groups: "real or perceived age, color, creed, national origin, race, religion, marital status, sex, sexual orientation, gender identity, physical attributes, physical or mental ability or disability, ancestry, political party preference, political belief, socioeconomic status, and familial status." (Iowa Department of Education 2011)

Schools are legally bound to take an unwavering stance against discrimination. A charge of harassment or discrimination can land your school district in court. This legal motivation, compounded with an intrinsic sense of right and wrong and an instinct to protect our students as would a parent, gives us the motivation and means to effect positive outcomes in schools and society.

Peaceful coexistence among groups is not easily attained. We have learned from and continue to be reminded of the violent and destructive history of slavery and civil rights in our country, and the tenacious persistence of bigotry. If the cure for intolerance and hatred were simple, it would have happened already. Changing an aspect of a culture, especially emotionally charged beliefs with a long and deeply rooted family and personal history, takes time and requires serious commitment and tenacity.

It also requires a heavy dose of two of the multiple intelligences identified by Howard Gardner: intra- and interpersonal skills, which ask us to consider ways of thinking that may be different from our own and to look past labels and quick judgments. We use our intrapersonal abilities to look inward, challenge our assumptions, and address our own prejudices. We use our interpersonal skills to open ourselves to new cultures and ideas, and to communicate and work harmoniously with others. Intrapersonal and interpersonal intelligence allow us to be comfortable with differences and socially adept at getting along.

IS IT BULLYING OR HARASSMENT?

Hate speech and racial, ethnic, and gender slurs are red flags for a lack of respect for groups of people based on a belief that you are better than they are and can treat them as you please, including violently. While we have students in our classrooms, part of our job is to prepare them to work and live in this diverse world. The attitudes they hold and choice of words they use are essential parts of their maturation into adults. Young children might use words or symbols of prejudice and hate without understanding their real meanings. A child may call someone *gay* or another slur, but, when asked, they do not truly understand the word. They are mimicking what they have heard. This is quite different from older children who know the meaning of what they are saying and that it is hurtful. Quick, calm intervention by an adult that includes a discussion of why the words or symbols are hurtful can stop the behavior.

Bullying is an act of violence committed repeatedly against a victim that escalates over time, and, sadly, through which the perpetrator appears to enjoy the power to intimidate and hurt. In a "Dear Colleague Letter" to all teachers across the country, Russalyn Ali of the Office for Civil Rights (OCR), part of the U.S. Department of Education, made a clear distinction between the generic term *bullying* and the more specific violence of *harassment* and *discrimination*. The OCR cautions educators to look at all aspects of the objectionable behavior to determine if it is bullying motivated by discrimination or hate for reasons of race, color, national origin, gender, age, or disability. If it is, this is a denial of guaranteed civil rights and a much more serious violation, which falls under the heading of harassment or discrimination.

The OCR is abidingly clear that a civil rights violation "necessitates schools to act beyond mere discipline of students. Schools need to eliminate hostile environments arising from the harassment, manage the effects of the harassment, and prevent the harassment from recurring." Among other measures, they recommend punishing the perpetrator, providing additional training to staff and students, reviewing and modifying school policies and the school code of conduct, and addressing the effects of the harassment by providing counseling, support, and protection for the victim. The OCR's bottom line recommendation is that school administrators and staff work to improve the climate of the school (Ali 2010).

Many think bullying is a catch-all phrase, one currently quite popular. In the National School Board Association article "Words Matter," author D. Nan Stein (2006) chastises us for our over use of the word bullying: "As children get older, bullying becomes an umbrella for a lot of misbehaviors, some of which are really 'criminal hazing or sexual/gender harassment' . . . But certainly by the time children are in the sixth grade, we ought to stop speaking in euphemisms or generalities."

The Anti-Defamation League (ADL) (2001) defines discrimination and harassment this way: "When people act on the basis of their prejudices or stereotypes, they are discriminating. Discrimination may mean putting other people down, not allowing them to participate in activities, restricting their access to work or to live in certain neighborhoods, or denying them something they are entitled to by right and law." The reality is that people are individually and culturally diverse, and we need to get along with others who are different from us. We should remind children that they can only dislike people they know; otherwise they have no good reason to not like them.

The ADL also warns of the ramifications of not responding to offensive words and behavior. If slurs are not addressed, this will lead children to believe that they are true, and that certain people deserve to be called names or to be disparaged.

An effective violence prevention plan responds immediately to comments and displays of intolerance and hate. It is important to make expectations clear—no name-calling or put-downs—and to model what we expect. In the book *Hate Hurts*, the ADL sorts into three categories the kinds of responses adults make to biased comments from children and young people:

Soft response—We ignore, avoid, and deny the problem and do not seek a solution. We stay uninvolved.

Hard response—We use confrontation, anger, and make verbal or physical threats. We try to win.

Principled—We communicate calmly, seeking understanding through dialogue, helping the child think through what happened, asking how they feel. We work toward solutions. (Stern-LaRosa and Bettman 2000, 184)

Every time we let a hurtful comment or act go by with no response we condone the behavior and undermine our own efforts. Every time we react with anger and impatience we model negative behavior. Every time we intervene appropriately we improve the climate and teach an expectation of tolerance.

Stern-LaRosa and Bettman offer the following examples of a principled response:

- "You just used a word in a way that was meant to be hurtful. Instead of telling Jose what he did that you didn't like, you called him a name" (199).
- If the child overhears name-calling and is concerned about it, an appropriate response would be: "Sometimes people call other groups names just to make themselves feel better or stronger, without always realizing how much it hurts" (198).
- If the child is the victim of bias, or you think he is, try this: "I hear that Michael is threatening some of the other Black kids. Has he done that to you?" (249)

"Six Steps to Speak Up," offered by Teaching Tolerance in response to hateful speech, says the first step is to always be ready to respond to offensive speech or behavior—to not "let bigotry win." It takes courage to act on a personal commitment not to turn the other way. Preparing a response ahead of time can boost our confidence to be vigilant.

THE STIGMA OF A PROGRAM

Many schools attempt to formally address issues of diversity under the heading of multicultural education. The term multicultural education is not always eagerly embraced, an example of the fallout of naming our efforts as stand-alone programs. It makes them easy objects of criticism when they do not bring quick results or they take too much time from academics. Also a problem is that the term multicultural is often interpreted as meaning "racial" and we have never been very good at facing issues of race in schools or society. If anything, we run from them out of a fear that we may not do it right or that it will cause further conflict, or because we have our own unresolved prejudices.

While we are passionately committed to bias-free schools, the label of "multicultural" or "character education" and its accompanying program activities can keep us from getting to the core of the issue. Following a pre-determined "curriculum" leads to a false sense of accomplishment: "I used the materials we were given, so I have done my part." We cover the particular multicultural, character education, or anti-bullying curriculum the school has adopted as if it were a unit on geometry or the Civil War. We then move on, never to address it again. Afterwards we can balk at a multicultural or character education curriculum and say it doesn't work and is too time-consuming, and that we *shouldn't teach it anymore*. Would we ever say the same thing about teaching math?

One way to avoid the pitfalls of programs is to describe rather than label our intentions. In reality, the goals of multicultural education are the same as for a safe school climate: to provide a healthy, equitable learning environment and challenging curriculum that prepare all students to lead peaceful and productive lives as citizens in a diverse democratic society. Multicultural education typically has three components: the development of attitudes, the acquiring of knowledge, and the mastery of life skills. At the minimum, it aims to teach tolerance of differences, while at a higher level it strives for understanding, acceptance, and ultimately appreciation and celebration of differences. By changing *multicultural education* to *safe school climate*, we can create a broad overarching effort that is less polarizing, and more accurate and approachable. In this way, respect for diversity takes on the highest priority as the foundation of a safe school climate and culture, and it reminds us that the climate is ours to create.

Respect for diversity is a broad concept that applies to both large demographic groups—racial, ethnic, gender, religious, socio-economic—and to the multitude of subcultures that exist in our schools. Sub-cultural groups may be organized around neighborhoods, sexual preference, common hobbies, academic performance, extracurricular activities, and social constructs such as clubs, gangs and cliques. These subcultures serve the basic human need to belong and give individuals a sense of identity; they also meet the need for power and fun and, in highly dangerous situations, for survival.

However, subcultures also serve to separate and alienate young people from each other, perpetuating parallel strands of students among which little interaction occurs. Schools are blessed with the opportunity, means, and motive to break down these barriers. The momentum can be tremendous when personnel are committed to both protecting students *and* bringing together students with various identifying labels. Exposure to others we once stigmatized or dismissed as lesser than us can reverse biased attitudes, reduce violence, and even build friendships.

No Tolerance? No Peace.

Ignorance ⇨Stereotypes ⇨Intolerance ⇨ Prejudice ⇨ **Violence**

OR

Ignorance ⇨Education ⇨Tolerance ⇨Acceptance ⇨ **Peaceful Coexistence**

THE CURRICULUM AND INSTRUCTION LINK

How do we teach the skills and attitudes of tolerance along with everything else we are expected to teach? Again, the answer lies in the egalitarian construct of compulsory public school attendance for all, which gives us daily access to students year after year.

What do we do with this precious time with students? How do we pay homage to the belief and mandate that all children have a right to a fulfilling education that culminates in graduation and preparation for a good life?

It varies by school and classroom. Some make issues of diversity a driving force of their teaching where it has reached the pinnacle of an embedded cultural tenet. Others pay little attention, especially if their school population is not racially or ethnically diverse. Since the school is considered "homogeneous" they assume they do not need to teach students to consider, respect, and to appreciate different cultures and perspectives.

This is unfortunate on two fronts. First, the truth is every school population is *diverse* merely by the uniqueness of each individual child attending the school. Many of the ways children find to discriminate against each other do not involve race or ethnicity, by instead focusing on socio-economic status, appearance, cliques, disabilities, sexual orientation, and family structure. It is naïve to think our students and their families are of a like mind, with equal status and power, and that everyone is treated respectfully. We recognize that some people enjoy more privilege than others. Second, the world is diverse and we live with the ramifications of ongoing conflicts between cultures and religions. All students benefit from school experiences that dispel stereotypes and prepare them to live and work harmoniously in a diverse society, and we know the best time to do this is when they are young.

In a good faith effort to be culturally sensitive schools create special focus days such "No Name-Calling Day." Worldwide awareness projects like "Pink Shirt Day" draw attention to the problem of bullying and harassment and make students feel they are part of a large group of social activists. These activities can reinforce our comprehensive safe schools climate efforts to respect diversity, but they should not be the focus of our effort. Every day should be no name-calling day. Changing climate and culture requires efforts with substance and ownership, and that are reinforced every day in the normal course of school life.

As with special days, individual teachers and whole schools might teach students about cultural and religious holidays to highlight and appreciate differences, and observe the designated special months—Black History, Women's History, Native American and Hispanic Heritage—to spotlight groups marginalized in American history and in the school curriculum. Activities designed to undo the legacy of discrimination are well intentioned and can raise awareness, but can also give us the false perception that we are meeting our obligation to make our school free of bias. If the principles of respect for and appreciation of diversity are not embedded into the curriculum and social climate, students will not internalize the necessary essential understandings about basic human rights and divergent histories. It takes a cohesive message and commitment for these concepts to take root.

Exemplary public school teachers welcome and serve every child as best they can. Regardless of whether we do or do not personally ascribe to some of the beliefs or practices of others, we realize our obligation to defend and champion each student's right to a bias- and intimidation-free learning environment.

Successful schools go beyond special days, months, and programs. They position respect for diversity at the core of their school climate efforts, and embed it in the curriculum, methods, and materials they choose for instruction. From pre-kindergarten through 12th grade, teachers who are committed to that philosophy strive to:

- Teach students to show tolerance and respect for each other within the learning environment.
- Be a positive role model for inclusion, respect, and empathy.
- Teach students to explore different cultural perspectives and points of view when evaluating historical and current events.
- Infuse a variety of cultures and perspectives into all aspects of the curriculum in an authentic way.
- Teach students the tools of problem solving through listening and speaking skills, conflict resolution, compromise, and consensus.
- Respond to acts of intolerance in a consistent and constructive way.
- Present students with opportunities to talk and work with those students they would not typically choose as a friend.

0%
Of seven widespread school programs designed to develop social and character development had an effect on student outcomes.
National Center for Education Research (2010)

HOW ARE DIVERSITY AND STANDARDS
INTERCONNECTED?

Instructional time is always an issue with teachers. There is never enough
of it. Broaching the subject of adding another topic or teaching strategy to
an already packed curriculum might not be received well. To complicate the
situation more, we exist under that ever-darkening cloud of standardized
assessments—a cloud that does not require that students pass a proficiency
test for tolerance and respect. But teachers and administrators can move it to
the top of the priority list where it belongs by learning how to embed respect
for diversity into the existing content of our curriculum, and by modeling it
in the way we teach and handle discipline.

Before looking at teaching strategies and changing attitudes, any effort
to improve school climate and build tolerance must begin with the violence
continuum activity described in chapter 3. Once we recognize that violence
does exist in our school, that it comes in many forms, and that students do not
learn well or at all when they are upset or afraid, we understand the central
importance of school climate. We embrace the idea that a safe and secure
climate helps all children meet their academic goals.

Then there are ingenious, yet simple, ways to implement a bias-free
classroom experience. A simple activity like a "standards search" helps
teachers discover how the spirit of teaching for diversity and good
citizenship is included in many of the academic standards for which we are
already responsible. To do the search at your school, arrange teachers in
small groups by grade level or content specialty. Distribute a copy of the
chart on the next page and provide copies of the learning standards for your
state.

Ask the teachers to look in the standards for references to knowledge,
skills, and attitudes that support the concept of respect for diversity and
appreciation of different cultures and perspectives. They will likely be
surprised to discover that these goals are a widespread and integral theme,
especially in social studies, a content area that is based on people's
perspectives and how they interpret what happened in the past.

For example, teachers in New York State would find that:

- The state English/Language Arts Learning Standards expect students to "respect the age, gender, and cultural traditions of all authors."
- The state Social Studies Learning Standards want students "to understand how different experiences, beliefs, values, traditions, and motives cause individuals and groups to interpret historic events and issues from different perspectives."
- The Learning Standards for Languages Other Than English want students to develop cross-cultural skills and understandings, and to draw comparisons between societies.

Respect for Diversity ⇦ ⇨ Learning Standards

How do the goals of teaching respect for diversity and state learning standards match up?

LEARNING STANDARD	KNOWLEDGE	SKILLS	ATTITUDES

GENERIC TEACHING STRATEGIES

Once we have identified how the goals of our curriculum include tolerance and appreciation for diverse groups, we can recognize the wisdom of choosing and developing instructional approaches that apply to many grade levels and many learning situations.

The more we perceive the life experiences of others as foreign or inferior to ours, the harder we need to work to see life through their eyes. There are many generic teaching strategies that emphasize considering and understanding the viewpoint of others without adding additional lessons, topics, or materials to use. They illustrate how, with a change of mindset, we can still cover the same curriculum in basically the same amount of time, but at a deeper level of understanding.

With these strategies we teach students to learn alongside a cross-section of people in a way that requires collaboration and teamwork. This personal contact breaks down the artificial barriers caused by ignorance, misconceptions, bias, and the other typical reasons that make students seek out or avoid certain students. Under the supervision of an observant and encouraging teacher who has set high expectations for positive behavior, students get to know each other as *individuals* instead of just members of a certain *group*. It is harder to victimize or demonize someone we have come to know as a real person.

The strategies that follow are easy to embed into the existing curriculum and are exemplary teaching methods:

- Have one student argue both sides of an issue.
- Have students take the other point of view on issues, events, and controversies.
- Arrange for students to interview each other and adults in the school about a specific issue or topic.
- Ask students to write a third person narrative of a personal experience and share it with the class.
- Provide students the opportunity to read and compare primary historical documents (e.g. journals, letters, diaries, political cartoons) and examine the context in which they were written.
- Read biographies and autobiographies, especially of risk takers who faced moral dilemmas.
- Share and use students' family heritages and traditions.
- Have students take on the persona of a character from literature or from history, and then role-play or write a journal entry showing how the character would view and respond to a current situation or event.
- Require students to compare/contrast historical perspectives using identifiable groups of people e.g. males/females, Europeans/Africans, factory workers/farmers.
- Research the time period when a book was written and look at how society might have influenced the author.
- Explore motives for decisions, acts, and laws.
- Write position papers and justify positions.
- Pose "What if the person did this instead" questions that give students decision-making power for people in history and literature.
- Hold regular Socratic dialogues in which students respond orally to a series of challenging questions by justifying their ideas, and listening respectfully to and working off of the ideas of others.

- Instruct using partners, cooperative learning groups, peer teaching, mixed-age groupings, and collaborative games.
- Use project-based learning related to community issues.
- Involve students in school and community service projects.

Over time these approaches teach students to be open-minded and to see things from multiple perspectives. They learn how membership in certain groups is defined by historical traditions, circumstances, and current events. Students go beyond stereotypes to viewing and evaluating others as individuals. Students are actively involved and expectations for them are high. This engaging teaching approach paired with caring relationships with students improves student behavior and the climate of the classroom, and in turn boosts academic achievement.

POOR SCHOOLS, MARGINAL TEACHING

Students tell us they want teachers who do not lecture, but instead provide "mutually respectful, trusting, engaging, interactive, and hands-on project-based student-centered learning" (Kohn 2011). Consider the kind of relationship a child can develop with a teacher who is calling out directions, moving along at a predetermined pace to cover a specific number of pages a day, who does not have time or inclination to answer questions, and limits interactions to paper and pencil work. Compare this to a learning climate where students explore rich concepts and understandings in a learner-centered setting.

The paradox is that the more vulnerable the children—urban, low-income, poorly funded schools, decaying neighborhoods, less educated parents—the more restrictive the curriculum and classroom management. There is little emphasis on decision making and high-level thinking skills, and group work and active engagement, the very things high-risk students need (Kohn 2011).

Intellectually stimulating experiences that teach children to consider the perspective of others and to work for the common good are unfortunately not the norm for all students. The National Assessment of Educational Progress (2010) has confirmed a disparity between how African American and White children are taught. Black children are more likely to be taught with workbooks and through rote memorization, a drumming in of basic skills, drill and practice, and bare-bones curriculum meted out in a strict classroom structure. Even the use of technology is geared to stimulus-response computer programs.

Much of this restrictive instruction is imposed on teachers to improve test results in under-performing schools. Scripted programs not only leave teachers little flexibility and insult their status as a professional, they also dehumanize students and interfere with our educational goal to develop good people. Students suffer when they do not have opportunities to practice social skills or explore information at a conceptual level. Giving students responsibility develops responsibility, recognizing positive behavior encourages positive behavior in the future, and asking students to think analytically makes them critical thinkers. A punitive, restrictive environment does none of this and is far from motivating.

In response to the argument that at-risk children need this kind of instruction, educator and author Alfie Kohn said, "Drill and skill instruction isn't how middle-class children got their edge, so why use a strategy to help poor kids catch up that didn't help middle-class kids in the first place?" (Kohn 2011) Consider how more affluent and educated parents would feel about this meager educational approach for their own children. Would they accept it or would they use their voice to challenge such practices?

WHAT ABOUT OUTSIDE SOURCES
OF INTOLERANCE AND HATE?

In the interactions between families and schools, it is inevitable that differences in beliefs will surface. How do we respond when a student's family creates a hateful or intolerant home environment that spills over into the classroom? What about issues stemming from religious beliefs? How do we stand strong against pressure from those who think parents alone should teach values and decide what children should and should not tolerate?

Public school teachers and administrators do not strive to undermine or question the teachings of parents, yet sometimes in the course of doing our work this happens. In public schools during the normal course of teaching a secular curriculum to a diverse community of students, we may delve into ideas and concepts that conflict with what children are learning at home. In some cases what we teach might even be in direct opposition to what the parents believe and teach to their children. Students may come from home to school with a deep-rooted prejudice that makes them feel entitled to demean and harass certain people. They might even be a member or sympathizer of a hate group.

In explaining why students might be attracted to such ideas, school social worker and diversity specialist Lillian Moss stressed one of the five basic needs, the need to belong. "Belonging to a group offers security, help with our daily responsibilities, and shared interests. It can be a source of pride and identity." The group could be the core family or an online site that draws in less self-confident young people who are alienated from their peers.

Teachers and principals always have to be prepared to defend challenges to our professional decisions, and we do this by being thoughtful in the selection of the content we teach and the materials we use. State education departments and local school boards and curriculum councils set the parameters (scope and sequence) for curricular content, and often for instructional practices and materials as well. Within the prescribed curriculum, teachers are free to challenge and motivate students in creative ways. As public school teachers we are protected if what we do and use to teach meets this two-pronged test: the material is based on the established curriculum and it is age-appropriate.

As discussed in chapter 1, society wants schools to help children become good citizens of strong character. We accomplish this by creating a school climate that actively protects the rights of each member. We implement a thought-provoking curriculum that encourages students to identify and analyze their assumptions about groups of people and to look at events and problems from multiple perspectives. While educators see these as the lofty goals that drive what happens in the classroom, parents might not be convinced.

We should always treat parents respectfully and if they challenge what is being taught, we should thank them for sharing their concerns or objections. We can learn a lot by being empathetic instead of defensive. Considering a parent's point of view keeps communication open and can establish a positive climate for discussion. Teachers and administrators should listen thoughtfully, tell parents they understand their concerns, and can explain how a particular topic or activity contributes to meeting the goals of a public education. It is important that parents be shown the state and local curriculum guidelines that confirm the concepts and content have been approved and are within educational expectations.

Surely parents have the right and are encouraged to discuss with their child what is taught in school, and to disagree and provide differing opinions. Differences between expectations at home and at school can coexist as long as the student participates fully in the curriculum and follows the school's expectations for tolerance and respectful behavior toward everyone.

A PROMISE TO PROTECT

We now see how public schools reflect the diversity in the general population, and that a public education is a great equalizing experience and that, by law, all children have a right to a free and appropriate education and more recently they are also guaranteed a safe, harassment-free school climate.

A vision of mutual respect can provide us with the will and stamina to address intolerance, discrimination, and challenges to our teaching. We promise children that we will protect their civil rights. We will not allow behavior that targets them because of their real or perceived race, ethnicity, religion, gender, or handicapping condition. Behavior that intimidates or robs them of their rightful place in the community is not okay in our school, and we will take action on their behalf. Such behavior is not okay even if it reflects family, religious, or individual cultural beliefs. With emotional and physical safety a priority, public school teachers and staff are obligated to stand up for victims of prejudice and violence with particular attention to behavior meant to harass and discriminate against an individual.

Equations That Add Up
Protection of rights + Consideration of
perspectives = Safer schools

Chapter 5

Is School Violence the Same for Everyone?

Sexual, racial, gender violence and other forms of discrimination and violence in a culture cannot be eliminated without changing culture.

—Charlotte Bunch

Those of us who have raised or work with children know they are preoccupied with the concept of fairness. They are indignant if they perceive a situation as unfair. They have not yet learned the disappointing lesson that life is not fair *or* unfair; it just is what it is. However within this randomness, good people still actively work to treat others fairly, make considered decisions, and stand up for others who are not being treated well. Life may not be fair, but we can create fair school policies and practices. We establish a foundation of fairness when we set expectations for behavior *and* keep an open mind as we address situations that arise, considering the act in the context of the situation.

When it comes to assessing school climate and the nature of violence in our school, it is important to be educated about the way violence develops and manifests itself in subcultures within the school community, the subcultures that provide context. In the previous chapter we discussed the rights guaranteed to all students, especially those groups protected by law because of a history of discrimination. We also learned how to structure the educational environment to instill a respect for diversity and meet academic goals for each child.

Children get teased, bullied, and harassed for being small, overweight, thin, having a learning disability, a speech impairment, the way they dress, their hygiene, their actual or perceived race, skin color, if they are poor, and increasingly for being gay. Children are picked on as they stand outside the school building, while waiting for the bus, on the walk or ride to school,

57

in hallways, the gym, bathrooms, classrooms, in the principal's office, and at recess and lunch. The potential is always there, especially if the school has allowed a disrespectful climate with no consequences for unacceptable behavior to develop.

ANTI-SOCIAL NETWORKING

The technological advances of the past few decades have increased the opportunity for bullying to occur. Cell phones and the Internet provide children with an emotionally distant, underhanded way to bully and humiliate others, and it is a way that follows the victim home. The seductive nature of electronic communication makes children feel no one is watching and can become a conduit for rumors, ganging up, and rejection.

The medium might be virtual, but the effect is not. People can express whatever is on their minds—what they think of another student, anger at a perceived slight, hatred for certain individuals or groups of people, or self-loathing. They can spread rumors and make violent threats against other people, groups, themselves, and the school community. Since these attacks are protected from the scrutiny of face-to-face encounters, social networking allows an individual to attack someone without looking them in the eyes, personal contact that might have triggered a feeling of empathy. The victim is left mortified, angered, or despondent.

Social networking adds to the anxiety and insecurity of adolescents as they worry about the number of friends they have on Facebook or fear someone is going to post something that will hurt them, something that will make it difficult to show their face in school. What used to be private or shared among a small group through gossiping on the phone and passing notes in school can easily be shared in public for anyone to see. Information about relationships is exposed or fabricated, and popularity and social status can come to seem like a competitive sport. (How many friends do you have on Facebook? Is that all?) Young people caught in the web of social intrigue should be taught how to cope with the negative face of social media, and be shown empathy for the very real trauma they are experiencing.

For those with a limited social group, the Internet breaks the isolation of being alone. It allows students to find others who share their beliefs—both healthy and unhealthy. Internet buddies and hate sites can validate and radicalize a student's hate-filled views and encourage him to take action. This is especially true in the middle school years, which are identified as the most physically violent and tumultuous period of child and adolescent development. Concerns about who they are and how they measure up to others breeds insecurity. In the downward spiral of "you hurt me so I must hurt you" and as I try to gain more power and status, this insecurity manifests itself in violent behavior meant to demean another person (Cybersafety n.d).

In response to five students accused of plotting a rampage at their Riverton, Kansas high school on the seventh anniversary of the Columbine massacre, James Garbarino posed the idea that "The Internet might be the reason why threatened school violence seemingly emerges in rural areas. The relative isolation makes rural youth rely on the Internet to a greater degree to stay connected to the greater youth culture" (Schultz and Williams 2006).

39%
Middle schools that reported student bullying occurred at school daily or at least once a week compared to 20% for primary and high schools. U.S. Department of Education (Neiman 2011)

The Tennessee State Legislature addressed the issue of harassment via social media with a July 2011 law that expanded the language defining harassment. It now includes anything that "communicates with another person or transmits or displays an image in a manner in which there is a reasonable expectation that the image will be viewed by the victim." To violate the law, and not be protected by the U.S. Constitution, exchanges have to be proven to be "malicious, frightening, intimidating or causing emotional distress to a victim." An important key to prosecution under this law is for the victim to have told the bully to stop, something we should advise all our students to do whenever they are bullied (Horton and Locker 2011).

As more states take a legal approach to cyber-bullying, parents and teachers need to pay close attention to children's use of the Internet and other social media. We need to show interest and make our presence known *while* children are using the Internet and cell phones. We need to bring up issues of personal safety and cyber-bullying and let our children know we are aware that hurtful things are done online. We can ask them about their own or their friends' experiences with social media and keep the dialogue going so they will come to us if something unsettling is said or done, or if a threat is made.

As in all safe school climate efforts, we must clarify the difference between tattling and reporting. We do not want to make children afraid to tell us something important because they might get in trouble for tattling. The difference lies in motive: Tattling is telling on someone to get them in trouble; reporting a problem is done to help yourself or others, a defense of dignity or in defense of personal safety. Role-playing scenarios with young children helps them see the difference between the two, and caring guidance along the way helps them decide when telling an adult is the right thing to do.

42%
6th–12th grade students who feel they
have personal power.
Search Institute Study, How Many Youth
Experience Each Asset? (2002)

TOXIC INFLUENCES

Children learn to use violent behavior, and can unlearn it. The challenge is greater the more severe their situation was. The nature, type, frequency, and intensity of the violence a child experiences depends on family environment and condition of neighborhoods, and the peers with whom they interact and associate. Exposure to extreme anti-social beliefs and normalization of violence in the home or on the streets affect a child's psyche. They acculturate him to accept and use the forms of violence he witnesses as a means of surviving his own circumstances. Anti-social behavior becomes the logical reaction to being treated violently, dominated, and discriminated against. It gives children a feeling of power when they have few ways to directly fight the injustices they face.

Ingrained violence from an abusive home life or violent neighborhood is resistant but not impossible to change. Early intervention efforts can be successful at leading students down a healthier path. An exception is the most dramatic example of this social-emotional dysfunction, the entrenched system of youth violence and criminal behavior of neighborhood gangs.

Everything about a gang is extreme. Gang membership is a way of belonging and is driven by an extreme sense of identity. Gang members act outside of the law using extreme measures to protect turf and retaliate against affronts. The gang expects an extreme level of loyalty from its members and is then extremely resistant to intervention. Their distorted views of human relationships and justice demand a more intense targeted intervention than the typical school efforts to make the school climate more respectful and inclusive. Resources designed specifically to address the particulars of gang life are critical and implementation requires highly skilled experts.

24%
Students polled who reported there were gangs at their schools.
CDC study (2008)

Gangs and violent hate groups are able to recruit vulnerable youth who are more susceptible to the promise of an identity, especially an identity to be feared. In response to a racially charged incident in a school, Lillian Moss told parents about the particular vulnerability of middle school age children:

> Obviously, the more insecure a young person is, the greater the need, and the more vulnerable they will be to a hate group's messages of superiority and anger. The group gives them a chance to belong, to feel important, and they may be willing to conform to demands that are questionable in order to be included. Nazi youth groups used group loyalty as a form of intimidation to force young people to perpetrate acts they might otherwise not do. The Klan groups, skinheads, and street gangs of today use similar tactics.

60%
Students polled who reported that within the previous year they were directly or indirectly, exposed to violence as a witness of violent acts or by overhearing threats made to someone close to them.
Child Trends: Children's Exposure to Violence (2010)

BEHAVIOR IN CONTEXT

Gender, race, grade, and neighborhood affect children's experiences and the 2009 Youth Risk Behavior Surveillance of U.S. students conducted by the Center for Disease Control evaluated the data they collected by these four sub-groups. The CDC's findings were vast and revealing. The survey found urban students were more likely to report problems with hostile remarks, physical fights, and gang violence, and they are more likely to have physical fights on school property than students in suburban and rural settings. Across all racial groups, girls reported more bullying than boys, and White boys have a higher rate of bullying behavior than African American and Latino males, who have more physical fights on campus.

Teachers and school staff are also victims of violence. Between 1999 and 2003, teachers were the victims of approximately 183,000 nonfatal crimes at school *every year*. This included 119,000 thefts and 65,000 violent crimes—rape, sexual assault, robbery, aggravated assault, and simple assault (Indicators of School Crime and Safety 2005). The way teachers are treated is a reflection of the violence in the students' home community that spills over into the schools.

Verbal abuse toward school adults is correlated to the size of the school; the larger the school the more verbal abuse teachers experience. In schools with over 1,000 students 26 percent of the principals who were surveyed reported teachers were verbally abused in their schools, compared to 14 percent of principals with 500–999 students, 10 percent of schools with 300–499 students, and 7 percent of schools with less than 300 students.

Male teachers were twice as likely as female teachers to be victims of violent crime, and the highest rate of student-to-teacher violence was found in high schools, followed by middle schools, and then elementary schools (Indicators of School Crime and Safety 2004).

Principals and teachers in these large urban, low socio-economic high schools and middle schools have their hands full when multiple factors converge. We have established that a student's life experiences and the type of community he lives in profoundly affect the understanding of what is and is not acceptable behavior. At times home and neighborhood provide a context for behavior that would be out of line in a school and, in the same way, school approved behaviors might seem foreign and impractical given the home environment. Children face an internal conflict in trying to live successfully in these two very different worlds.

This results in the alienation of students who are raised in toxic environments and find themselves in a school culture that contradicts their own norms. They get in trouble more easily and more frequently for using the survival skills they have adopted in response to a culture of violence where emotional and physical force is the everyday means of dealing with conflict. Their behavior is as much about self-preservation as it would be for a soldier in a war zone, but the behavior is still serious and must be stopped.

FROM NEEDS TO...

Child's needs not met ⇨

Frustration sets in ⇨

Lacks the pro-social skills needed to get needs met ⇨

Chooses angry, hurtful behavior ⇨

TROUBLE

FROM NEEDS TO...

Child's needs not met ⇨

Concern sets in ⇨

Has the pro-social skills needed to get needs met ⇨

Chooses peaceful, constructive behavior ⇨

RESOLUTION

ONE SIZE DOES NOT FIT ALL

With our broad understanding of violence as a continuum of behaviors, we are better prepared to address violence in all its forms and to understand its patterns. We have the opportunity to be compassionate and fair in our expectations, and work with students to replace their learned violent behaviors with socially acceptable alternatives, each according to need. The more alienated the student, the greater the feeling of powerlessness and the greater the effort needed to reach out to help him develop that critical missing connection to the school and to those in it.

We have a responsibility to treat individual students in the way that is most effective for them, meeting them where they are, helping them grow in self-discipline and self-control to get their needs met. We consider context and understanding of individual circumstances but do not excuse or ignore violent or destructive behavior. Everything is addressed, standards are kept high, and safety of students and staff remains the top priority.

In contrast, inconsistent responses to acts of violence and " zero tolerance" policies that react rigidly to categories of behavior cause students and families to regard school rules and staff with skepticism, seeing them as unresponsive and even discriminatory. They lose faith in the educational system, or see their preconceived opinions about the school being reinforced. These missteps undermine our efforts to build the trust needed to change behavior.

Such missteps include the zero tolerance policies that were enacted in the 1990s as a response to a growing concern about the presence of illegal drugs, alcohol, and firearms on school campuses. The Gun Free Schools Act of 1994 implemented a nationwide law mandating a one-year expulsion for students who were proven to have brought a firearm or other weapon to school. Over time some states and school districts expanded zero tolerance policies to include a wide range of behaviors including illegal drugs, insubordination, and bullying.

Unfortunately researchers have found that such punitive threats do little to deter violent behavior and often exacerbate a problematic situation. Automatic rigid penalties such as suspensions and expulsions:

• Prevent schools from considering context and individual circumstances.
• Are disproportionate to race and socio-economic status.
• Encourage adults to give up on problem students.
• Do nothing to encourage interventions that could help change students' behavior, save them from dropping out of school, and keep them from continuing to act violently.
• Can look foolishly misguided as in examples of the suspension of a kindergarten child for bringing a weapon to school (a dinner knife), or a first grader for sexually harassing a classmate (kissing her during recess).

A comprehensive policy research report on the effect of zero tolerance policies and practices found "an almost complete lack of evidence that zero tolerance is among the strategies capable of accomplishing that objective (reducing violent and illegal behavior). The researchers concluded, "one can only hope for the development and application of more effective, less intrusive alternatives for preserving the safety of our nation's schools" (Skiba 2000).

School education lawyer Dean Pickett understood the concept of context when he called for a more reasonable approach, which involves "zero tolerance for behavior but not zero thinking" (Hutton 2006). The addition of

42%
Students expelled for violation of the Gun
Free Schools Act who were from elementary
and middle schools.
Child Trends: Results to Research Study
by Boccanfuso and Kuhfeld (2011)

thinking allows administrators to consider context and circumstances, and
intent and prior history of the student to determine the most fair and effective
response.

It is a challenge to teach children the skills they need to stop choosing
negative behavior when many of them do not have the emotional security
required to make healthy choices. Instead of nurturing, trusting, and consistent
relationships with loving adults, they have a hyper-vigilant emotional
foundation that comes from a variety of factors, including a life of neglect,
abuse, family conflicts, poverty, substance abuse, and unsafe neighborhoods.
A vicious cycle revolves around the insecurity of their personal situation,
which makes them more distrustful and susceptible to the culture of violence,
which then leads to harmful behaviors that only perpetuate the lack of
emotional security.

In this environment, many young people develop a matter-of-fact view of
violence and death. They might not think what they are doing is wrong or
understand what they are being asked to do instead; it conflicts with what
they know to be true in real life. To protect themselves they respond the best
they can to the harsh lessons they learn early in life. Without the social bonds
and trust that come from a safe and caring family and with many of their
basic needs not met, children fight to survive in unhealthy violent ways. The
resulting coping mechanisms persist into adulthood.

Dr. James Garbarino, in *Lost Boys*, describes the background of men on
death row this way:

> Each of these men had been subjected to extreme child maltreatment,
> yet none received mental health treatment once that victimization was
> substantiated by the state child protective services agency. I could not help
> but think that if any one of these young men had been taken hostage by a
> terrorist group and tortured for years, there would have been no question
> about their need for and entitlement to mental health services upon their
> release. Yet we did not provide the same services to these 'hostages' once

they were released from their tormentors. And now we intended to execute them" (Garbarino 1999, 191).

One size does not fit all when we consider that young people's anti-social and self-destructive behavior, such as gang membership, depression and drug use, vandalism or theft, and early sexual behavior is an understandable reaction to a life of neglect and abuse. Targeted early intervention with mental health professionals is essential when a child's anti-social behavior is a reaction to coping with a personal life of pervasive violence. This is where the school, more than ever, needs to be a safe haven where the negative forces of a child's life outside the school do not carry over into the educational environment.

Research shows that two thirds of students living in dire conditions rise above and succeed in spite of their circumstances. What does this two thirds have that the other one third is missing? We can prevent or mitigate the negative effects of a high-risk childhood by providing these assets that build the network of support and the personal resilience that are characteristic of survivors of toxic environments. These assets benefit all children but are critical for the most vulnerable, and include:

- Caring relationships.
- High expectations.
- Meaningful participation.
- Autonomy and sense of self.
- Sense of meaning and purpose.
  (California Healthy Kids Survey 1999)

A study on the relationship between student and teacher safety and the nature of the school and home community in the Chicago Public Schools found this to be true (Steinberg et al. 2011). Controlling for academic achievement and type of neighborhood (crime and poverty levels), the schools with the highest suspension rates were less safe than those with low suspension rates. Researchers discovered that the neighborhood in which the school was located was not as influential as the students' home neighborhood. The primary difference between schools that felt safe and those that did not was the quality of the relationships between school staff and students and parents. The study concluded, "disadvantaged schools with high-quality relationships actually feel safer than advantaged schools with low-quality relationships."

In addition, the report noted that a relationship exists between student low academic achievement and increased problems with school safety and order.

Schools with a population of low-achieving students experience higher rates of violence. This finding supports growing research that recommends schools focus on raising the literacy rates of young children, adolescents, and adults to reduce violence in schools and in the community (Jalloh 2009). Research on aggressive behavior, high school dropout rates, crime, incarceration and recidivism, unemployment, and poverty show a positive correlation between these negative outcomes and poor literacy skills, especially among Latino and African American males. The literacy-violence connection has been widely documented and the results show this aggression begins in the primary grades when children first experience frustration when trying to learn to read.

To succeed at academics, students need *cognitive confidence* (ability to read fluently with comprehension), *text confidence* (stamina to read increasingly difficult material), and *social and emotional confidence* (positive attitude and enjoyment of reading) (Jalloh 2009, 3). Students who have many negative risk factors in their lives need an intentional school support system and targeted early intervention efforts to teach literacy, math, and technology skills. Without this support these children become disengaged underachievers who stop trying, turn to violence to get what they need, leave school before they graduate, and live a life of poverty and crime. This reality reinforces the need for school-wide, intentional efforts to improve the interactions and relationships among staff, children, and families, and make the connection to academic success.

Teachers know we can intervene early and change this pattern. The Chicago Public Schools study gives credence to the belief that the way we relate to our students is the critical factor in reducing school violence and improving academic performance. A secure climate is necessary for children to take risks and learn. It is in our power to create a secure, caring climate that addresses the academic and social-emotional needs of our students and builds resilience against negative circumstances, regardless of their neighborhood of origin.

THE INFLUENCE OF GENDER ROLES

Without thinking, we tend to think of boys when we talk about violence. This is especially true when we hold a narrow view of what violence looks like. But friction and conflict are a normal part of everyone's life in general, and of interpersonal relationships in particular, and we know conflict often leads to aggression.

How do girls and boys respond to life's conflicts? What assets do they have to guide them to choose healthy solutions to problems? Males and females respond to conflict the way societal norms and their families have taught them to respond. The influence of gender on the kinds of violence they use comes from stereotypes and pressure from rigid male and female roles. Social norms still drive what is acceptable male and female behavior in spite of the strides made in the past fifty years that identify many gender differences as social constructs rather than biological imperatives. Though gender expectations do vary some by racial and ethnic cultures, the dominant American culture puts all young people of both sexes at risk for different kinds of pain and suffering.

Research on gender norms reveals what we might have suspected: boy-to-boy violence is more physical, noisy, obvious, and difficult to ignore. Boys are more likely to join gangs and hate groups, and to use overt forms of violence than are girls. The paradox is that this aggressive behavior is a socially expected and accepted gender norm for boys. *Boys will be boys* is a compliment said with a wink and a smile. Maybe it is not surprising that the perpetrators of all school shootings in the past two decades have been White males.

If females intended to damage the social culture of the school on such a grand scale, the violence they used would likely look very different. In her groundbreaking book, *Odd Girl Out*, Rachel Simmons exposed the hidden, but very real, types of *alternative aggression* girls use to manipulate and dominate other girls. She says, "Our culture refuses girls access to open conflict, and it forces their aggression into nonphysical, indirect, and covert forms" (Simmons 2002, 3).

While female perpetrated violence from the more overt, physical end of the continuum has grown over the past few decades, girl-on-girl violence still remains primarily relationship-based. Girls tend not to respond to persistent bullying in the overtly violent and even deadly ways boys do. They suffer their devastation in silence, keeping the hurt inside. Latina, African American, and White girls all have significantly higher rates of feeling sad and hopeless than boys, and twice as many girls as boys attempt suicide (National Youth Risk and Behavior Surveillance Survey 2010).

Simmons sums up the gender difference this way: When faced with conflict boys are more apt to choose "fight or flight while girls choose to tend and befriend." What does this tending and befriending look like when there is conflict? Female aggression typically is driven by the basic need to belong and is more personal than male aggression. Therefore, girls do not easily rebound from disagreements and conflicts. Female violence designed to manipulate relationships is typically subtle but emotionally devastating and referred to as *mean*. If someone says *girls will be girls*, it is with a shake of the head and is not a compliment.

To maintain their position of power, status, and popularity, girls use "backbiting, exclusion, rumors, name-calling, and manipulation to inflict psychological pain on targeted victims" (Simmons 2002, 3). Girls destroy relationships, a very potent way to wield power against each other. Since the relationship between boys is typically not an intimate one, boys tend to take conflicts less personally. Boys may act out in a noisier way by starting

60%
Boys who were identified as bullies in middle school who had at least one criminal conviction by the age of twenty-four.
CDC Study (2008)

physical fights or fighting back, but they rebound from altercations more quickly than girls.

It is evident that neither girls nor boys go unscathed by these stereotypes. The pressure is on to protect your male toughness or your female softness. Feminine attributes are used as slurs to taunt and shame boys because they infer weakness. Being told you do something or sound "like a girl" is a putdown. Male attributes are seen as strong and desirable, and in slang both genders are told to "man up" when they need to show some backbone.

Boys are made to feel entitled to be in charge and to use overt power to get their needs met. Girls feel less entitled to have and show power so they meet their needs in less direct ways. This may not be unexpected in a male-dominated society where women did not get the right to vote until 1920, after a seventy-two year campaign.

Think of the violence continuum and some of the behaviors at the subtle end. You will recognize them as the more "female" methods of inflicting violence on others; they are the quiet and more socially accepted and ignored ways they gang up against each other. The target of female bullying loses the thing most precious to her—her relationships with her friends—without a voice being raised or a punch thrown. No adult intervenes because it happens quietly and does not draw any attention. No one was yelling or shoving or "got hurt." Within the quiet intrigue of friendship and social status, adults often miss this aggression altogether, or if we do notice, we consider it to be a benign part of female relationships.

While female aggression continues to slowly edge into the male realm of physical violence, new developments in gender based relational aggression show the reverse is also true. Female peers increasingly draw boys into this psychological terrorism as targets or participants. Simmons reports that research has uncovered ". . . a shrinking gender gap in behaviors like relational aggression, especially by middle school. Adolescent boys are telling researchers that relational and social aggression—actions that damage friendship and reputation—concern them more than physical intimidation" (Simons 2011). This is most evident in the turbulent middle school years.

When teachers ignore the meanness and gossiping associated with typical "mean girl" behavior, we condone this use of violence and the serious threat it poses to the mental and emotional health of our students. Missed, dismissed, underestimated and less frequently pursued and punished, relational aggression then escalates. If adults downplay a disagreement or tell a girl who reports the meanness to stop tattling or not to be so sensitive, we deny that females use relationships to hurt others. As Simmons so wisely observes, "teachers are hardly breaking down the door to discipline behavior that is usually as invisible as it is" (Simmons 2002, 226). The result is the accumulation of self-doubt and isolation that can lead to depression among girls, and for boys, reporting this type of typically female violence would be to the detriment of their status as a strong male and only likely expose them to more bullying.

To be fair, there is a strong likelihood that most teachers do not understand relational aggression themselves. Both males and females might never have learned to handle conflict in a direct and positive way; very few of us have. After an exploration of bullying and relational aggression, graduate students in my gender issues in education class (overwhelmingly female) recognized times in their lives when they were involved in such a situation. Some have emotional scars and some hold grudges to this day. After our discussion, one student even reached out to the girl she had bullied more than a decade ago to ask for forgiveness.

The class suggested these tips for teachers to reduce relational aggression in their schools:

- Be more educated; know what to look for.
- Have open communication with students.
- Be more aware of students' body language.
- Don't downplay incidents; acknowledge them.
- Use role-playing to provide examples of situations, with possible responses and consequences.
- Teach conflict resolution.

GAY-BASHING AND SOCIAL CHANGE

"In the hierarchical, awkward battleground that is junior high lunch period, Larry King was deployed as a weapon. The 'losers' ate inside the cafeteria, and the 'cool kids' ate outside near the basketball courts—and that is where King was used" (Barlow 2011). Some of the girls in Larry King's class would goad him to ask to sit at the cool kids' table, hoping to get a reaction from the students sitting there. The asked him to do this again on February 11, 2008, and the next morning, while Larry was sitting in the computer lab of his Oxnard, California middle school, Brandon McInerney, one of the cool kids, shot Larry twice in the back of the head. Larry was fifteen years old and openly gay.

The discussion of gender stereotypes and groups who experience violence in a less typical way leads us to the very real problem of homophobia and the manifestation of such hate in gay-bashing. Brandon McInerney is now seventeen and facing a retrial for the murder of King. The first trial, where he was treated as an adult, and charged with first degree murder and a hate crime, resulted in a hung jury.

How common is harassment of lesbian and gay individuals in our society? Mark Potok calculated the percentage of the general population of each of six categories (homosexuals, Jews, Blacks, Muslims, Latinos and Whites) and compared this to the number of hate crimes aimed at each group. The results were sobering: Homosexuals were victimized 8.3 times the expected rate given their percentage of the population. This disproportionate likelihood of victimization was compared to the other groups and revealed that gay individuals were:

- 2.4 times more likely to be the target of a hate crime than Jews
- 2.6 times more likely than Blacks
- 4.4 times more likely than Muslims
- 13.8 times more likely than Latinos
- 41.5 times more likely than Whites (Potok 2010, 29)

Violence toward students who are gay, or are perceived to be gay, is part of the school bullying behavior that crosses the line to harassment and discrimination by infringing on the civil rights of a protected group. The Southern Poverty Law Center offers a stirring video and study guide free to educators. *Bullied* tells the story of Jamie Nabozny, the victim of anti-gay

90%
Of the 7,261 middle and high school lesbian, gay, bi-sexual, and transgender students surveyed who reported harassment at school in the past year. GLSEN Survey (2009)

violence that started in middle school. The harassment moved along the continuum from teasing, name-calling, and taunting, to stalking, threats, and brutal physical attacks. The building principal's solution? He told Jamie he should stop acting so gay.

After years of changing schools and reporting incidents to school authorities with no satisfaction, Jamie and his parents eventually fought back and sued the school and the building administrators for not protecting Jamie even though they were aware he was being victimized. The outcome was the groundbreaking court ruling that school personnel must protect the students in their care from violence. It is their moral *and* legal responsibility.

In an article about the film, one teacher who showed *Bullied* to her class reported the students were absolutely silent during the video and long after it ended (Kurzweil 2010, 25). It is that powerful. Showing this video to adults and middle and high school students can be an essential part of any safe school effort. While at times upsetting to watch (when you feel empathy, seeing someone be victimized *is* uncomfortable), the dose of reality is worth the discomfort. You and your students will not be the same once you have seen it.

Bullied can be the catalyst for a serious discussion of bullying and harassment, understanding the roles students and adults play in this kind of violence, and changing attitudes toward violence aimed at gays or any group. It can trigger feelings of empathy and compassion. The importance of this reeducation is heightened when we learn that two thirds of lesbian, gay, bi-sexual, and transgender (LGBT) students feel unsafe because of their sexual orientation, and almost a third have skipped at least one day of school in the previous month because of safety concerns (GLSEN 2009).

8
Number of states that currently have statewide legal protections for students based on sexual orientation. GLSEN Study (2006)

We are currently in a period of a civil rights struggle by the LGBT community. As people push back against social changes they see happening and do not welcome, negativity and violence toward the group escalates, making it especially important to be aware and proactive. This was the situation after the 1954 Supreme Court decision in *Brown v Board of Education* that separate but equal schools were unconstitutional and schools could no longer be segregated by race. The desegregation of America's public schools faced staunch opposition in many areas, opposition that was often violent and supported by elected officials. While prejudice against African Americans has dissipated since then, it has not disappeared. Yet it is now the law that no one can interfere with an African American child's right or any other child's right to attend a public school.

20%
Students with disabilities who received a public education in 1970.
Briefing Paper National Council on Disabilities by Young et al. (2011)

SPECIAL NEEDS, SPECIAL CARE

Students who stand out in some way are preferred targets for bullies. This is especially true of students with special needs who are harassed because of their appearance, speech, behaviors, and communication or social skills. Federal Civil Rights legislation in 1975 made an about-face in how and where students with disabilities were taught. The court ruled all children were entitled to a free and appropriate education in the least restrictive environment, and those with special needs came back from special schools, institutions, and separate classes in separate buildings to join the local public school system. The least restrictive placement often meant a self-contained special education class in a public school building, which created negative attitudes toward "special ed kids." For many classified students this has evolved to mean inclusion and mainstreaming into general education classes and improved academic and social development and acceptance and understanding by their peers (Young et al. 2011, 73).

This shift has also, however, led to a silent epidemic of corporal punishment, social exclusion, and bullying at a higher rate than for other students. Young, an expert on special needs students, writes, "Bullying is every parent's fear. For children with special needs that fear is exacerbated. . . . It became apparent that the demographic most vulnerable to bullying also had the fewest resources."

The web resource, "Walk a Mile in Their Shoes: Bullying and the Child with Special Needs," gives accounts of actual harassment as told by parents of and children with special needs. Such dignity-robbing and physically dangerous violence included a Facebook hate page set up to ridicule a student, tying a child to the playground fence using his sweatshirt and posting a video on Facebook of him trying to get free, pinning down a child and forcing him to eat dog food, repeatedly spiking a student's lunch drink with alcohol, and punching and shoving a child and knocking her off her crutches (Young n.d., 3–7). The organization, Ability Path, was developed in response to a glaring need for an online community for parents and professionals concerned about the issue, saying it was time to take back our schoolyards and the Internet and make them safe, especially for special needs children who are more vulnerable and targeted more often.

94%
Middle class mothers of students with Asperger's Syndrome (high functioning autism) who reported peers were victimizing their child. Issues in Pediatric Nursing Survey by Little (2002)

Parents and school professionals need information like this, especially since schools are required to prevent and respond forcefully to discrimination based on disability the same as they would for any bias-based violence toward the other federally protected groups. This group of students requires more targeted bullying awareness and prevention efforts than what might be presented to the general school population.

One way to be proactive and ensure this will happen is to include approaches to discipline, development of social skills, and self-advocacy instruction in the child's Individualized Education Plan (IEP). Massachusetts passed legislation in 2010 requiring that IEPs address equipping students with specific skills to avoid being bullied (Young et al. 2011, 77). Of course, this practical step in self-protection must be coupled with a nurturing, bias-free school climate where everyone is accepted and targeting certain groups for teasing, bullying, and harassment is strictly prohibited. If students with disabilities are disproportionately targeted for violence, efforts to protect these children need to be proportionately strong and send a clear message of what will not be tolerated.

ATHLETES: A PROTECTED CLASS?

Double standards are not a new form of discrimination in life or in schools. Historically race, ethnicity, socio-economic status, and social connections affect how you are viewed and treated. Participation in organized sports encourages positive behavior and can build personal assets including goal setting, determination, hard work, self-discipline, teamwork, and hopefully good sportsmanship.

However, athletes also have status, especially in the high-profile male sports like football, soccer, wrestling, and basketball, and it is not uncommon for schools and society to give them special dispensation when they break the rules. Athletes provide entertainment, build school pride, and bring prestige to the school and their violent behaviors and rule breaking are sometimes excused. The attitudes of teachers, administrators, and parents who believe participation in sports is always a character-building experience perpetuate the treatment of the "athlete as a privileged class."

While the majority of athletes do not abuse their popular status, this privileged "jock culture" gives many athletes an overblown sense of importance and entitlement, and the physical and social dominance that comes with it. The *Teaching Tolerance* article, "Jock Privilege," claims it leads to athletes who sometimes "feel they have permission to dominate the social organization of the school . . . in a variety of ways, usually claiming space in hallways and in cafeteria lines, and taking opportunities in some classes to demean other students, enhancing their own status in the process" (Jock Privilege n.d.). Being idolized, feared, admired, and envied for athletic skills and brute force do not build character. They breed idolatry and a sense of entitlement that can lead to abuses of power and status.

Complicating the issue are coaches who that think breaking down an athlete's self-esteem by verbally belittling him or handing out physical punishment is an effective way to motivate him to try harder. In this way, coaches openly model aggressive bullying behavior. As states and districts enact measures to reduce bullying by athletes, coaches who bully are under more scrutiny for their own violent behavior. They are being told to tone down their drastic discipline techniques and to no longer look the other way when one of their athletes bullies another student.

Parents and school adults have the power to turn around this injustice, just as we have the power to correct any injustice that exists under our watch. "Jock Privilege" offers some examples of positive actions coaches can take. T. J. Mills, head football coach at Permian High School in Odessa, Texas is a good example of a coach who takes being a positive role model seriously. Mills believes it is so important to teach his athletes positive character traits for behavior on and off the field that he regularly leads his teams in thirty-minute "Character Development Sessions." His driving belief is that coaches must also coach athletes to be socially responsible.

To the same end, Mark Calhoun, head football coach of Denver East High School encourages his players to get involved in nonathletic school activities where their exposure to students with whom they normally do not socialize builds respect and understanding for nonathletes.

And promising initiatives, where athletes use their influence to take a stand against bullying, have sprung up all over the country. Creating a climate where bullying is not okay, including by athletes, has the potential to have a dramatic positive effect on the climate and culture of public schools.

VIOLENCE IS GROUP-SPECIFIC

Violence does not look the same and is not motivated by the same forces for all groups. It is influenced by the nature of families and neighborhoods, choice of friends, gender, sexual identity, race and ethnicity, disability, privilege, and special status. We can reduce violent influences by having a clear definition of violence, and of what is and is not allowed at our school, while also considering contributing factors, including the context in which the violence occurs.

Students lacking secure and nurturing personal lives need asset-building experiences that develop personal empowerment. Victimized youth need positive interventions to build resilience against the violence heaped on them. Girls, and now boys, need to be taught about relational aggression and how to resolve conflicts constructively. Adults need to take a stand against special status for athletes. Children with disabilities need to be taught social skills and actively protected from harassment. These efforts and the school's compassion help both victims and perpetrators overcome and reject the effects of negative family experiences, socio-economic circumstances, social pressures, and gender issues.

Equations That Add Up
Expectations + Context = Fair outcomes for all

Chapter 6

What Are the Elements of a Safe School Climate?

Whether we permit chance environments to do the work, or whether we design environments for the purpose makes a great difference. And any environment is a chance environment so far as its educative influence is concerned unless it has been deliberately regulated with reference to its educative effect.

—John Dewey

You park your car in a spot that is marked "visitors" and walk to the closest door. It is locked, so you walk around to the main entrance. You notice a resource officer standing outside the building, interacting with a few stragglers coming late to school. He tells you the front door is the only entrance not locked to the outside once school is in session.

You read the notice on the door welcoming you to the school and directing you to sign in at the main office. You walk into the school and one of the first things you notice is how bright and colorful the lobby is. There is a cluster of live plants and a banner with a positive school code of conduct draped along the wall. A large bulletin board displays an encouraging message about being considerate toward each other and is decorated with student illustrations. Another bulletin board stresses no tolerance for bullying and how getting help for someone being hurt is not tattling; it is the right thing to do. Posters, murals, and artwork on the walls show young people and adults of all races and genders in all kinds of school, family, and work situations.

A receptionist sitting at the table in the front hallway asks if he could help and directs you to the main office next door. The friendly school secretary gives you a visitor's pass, which clearly indicates your name, the date, and your destination. You clip it to your jacket.

As you walk down the hall, teachers and staff members make eye contact and say hello. Everyone is wearing a photo ID and they glance at your visitor's pass. You get confused trying to find the social studies' classroom and ask a passing student for help. She says, sure, and escorts you all the way to the room. You thank her for being so kind and she says you are welcome, that students at this school are supposed to be helpful.

You knock on the classroom door, and the teacher waves for you to come in. The students have been studying our continental neighbors to the north and to the south and are expecting you. The teacher introduces you to the class. He explains that you are a friend of his who is going to share what it was like growing up in rural Mexico, moving to Mexico City for college, and eventually settling in the United States. He reminds the students to listen respectfully and to handle carefully the materials you brought in to share with them. The children are engaged and ask thoughtful questions, many of which they had brainstormed earlier. They are well prepared for your visit and do not laugh at unfamiliar Mexican names, traditions, or clothing, and enjoy the Mexican wedding cookies you brought for them to try. The students give you a round of applause when you finish and thank you for coming. The teacher shakes your hand and asks if you will come back next year.

Classes are changing as you head back to the office to sign out. You see teachers standing at their classroom doorways saying hello to children by name and gently reminding them to pick up any litter they drop. The older students are coming to the cafeteria for lunch. Cafeteria aides stand ready to supervise them in line and as they choose a place to sit. An aide notices a new child standing alone with his tray. She introduces him to a small group of students in his grade and asks if he can join them. They say yes and make room for him on the bench.

As you reach the office it is busy with teachers checking their mailboxes and grabbing a homemade cookie or two from the tray left for them by the PTA. A few students are there to pick up notices for their teachers and to visit the nurse for their noon medications. The secretary answers the phone with a cheerful voice, giving her name. A parent comes in to sign out her child for a dentist appointment and is shown to a comfortable chair as she waits.

You sign out on the visitor's log and return your visitor's badge. As you head toward the front door you realize that the building is quiet but not silent, orderly but not stifling, lively but not hectic. The floors are free of trash, and the air smells good from the lunch the kitchen staff is cooking. You say goodbye to the receptionist and, as you go out the door and nod to the resource officer, you find yourself feeling peaceful and looking forward to the day you will return.

AUDITING THE CLIMATE

You have just completed an informal school climate audit, an objective view of a school campus. You came away with an assessment of building security, relationships between students and adults, the school and families, and what is taught and valued. Your impression of security measures and the school climate is favorable.

Over the past decade, in response to the tragic student-on-student assaults at Columbine and other schools, states have mandated that school districts follow specific guidelines to make and keep their campuses safe, including conducting security and climate audits. All states have school safety requirements and 45 out of the 50 have specific anti-bullying laws. As John Dewey said, if you want to make a specific change in your environment you need to be intentional in your efforts.

Typical of the legislated plans is the New York State S.A.V.E. (Schools Against Violence in Education 2000) mandate, which specifies that every school district must address violence through:

1. District-wide safety plans.
2. Building-level emergency response plans.
3. Codes of conduct.
4. Teacher authority/Principal authority guidelines.
5. A Uniform Violent Incident Reporting (UVIR) system.
6. Instruction in civility, citizenship, and character education.
7. Health curriculum.
8. Interpersonal violence prevention education.
9. School violence prevention training.
10. Whistle blower protection (Project SAVE 2000).

The State of New Jersey's "Anti-Bullying Bill of Rights" signed into law in January 2011 revised and supplemented their existing laws on harassment, intimidation, and bullying in public schools, to make them the most comprehensive in the country. Legislators expanded the definition of these forms of violence to include "the creation of a hostile environment for the student by interfering with a student's education or by severely or pervasively causing physical or emotional harm to the student" (NJ P.L. 2010. c.122 [A-3466]). New Jersey has formally codified the connection between the climate of the school and the quality of student learning and has acted on this understanding.

The New Jersey law also formalizes staff training. By the 2012–13 school year, all candidates for school administrator or school teacher licensing must complete a training program on harassment, bullying, and intimidation prevention, and now the state *requires*, no longer just *encourages*, schools to establish bullying prevention "programs" or "approaches." The approaches must include, among other requirements, suicide prevention education for teachers and a uniform reporting system for incidents of prohibited behavior witnessed by a staff member. Also included in the mandate is a protocol for investigating complaints against the school. The law states that, "each school district must form a safety team in each school in the district to foster and maintain a *positive climate* within the schools." New Jersey legislators reaffirmed the inseparable link between the violence continuum and school climate.

All educators of every state care about school safety, yet the most conscientious schools are proactive in addressing and reducing violence at all points on the continuum. They know their student population and how to improve the climate of their school. Administrators, teachers, and staff look at themselves honestly and consider their own beliefs, and then evaluate and modify their practices.

Members of a proactive school have efficacy—they believe they have the power to make the changes needed to create a violence-free climate for learning. In these schools every adult is responsible for *all* students, not just those they teach. Families are actively engaged and treated with respect and viewed as valuable partners in their children's academic and social-emotional growth. School personnel ask for, listen to, and act on parents' ideas and concerns. If the need arises there is an emergency plan everyone in the school has practiced and an active school crisis management team in place.

1,634
Number of U.S. high schools considered "dropout factories" where less than 60% of the students graduate on time.
Five Promises Study (2009)

ENGAGING AND SUPPORTING STUDENTS

A primary challenge in creating a positive school climate is getting students engaged. A 2011 Gallup Poll found that only half of students in grades

5–12 are "engaged" in school, engaged being defined as highly involved and enthusiastic, with the other half "going through the motions" and doing things to intentionally undermine their classroom climate. We must do something to draw in the students we are losing. Student engagement happens through meaningful experiences, a collective identity and sense of belonging, emotional safety, an understanding of cause and effect, and taking responsibility for your own behavior. And it also happens through academic success. It is critical that we get students reading successfully in the primary grades and help them internalize positive attitudes toward school, personal effort, and academic achievement.

Prevention efforts reject the *psychology of failure* that stresses comparison and competition, uses public shaming and punishments as consequences, and offers only extrinsic rewards. The foundation of prevention is a safe school plan that focuses on positive development of social skills and attitudes through a *psychology of success* (Shindler et al. 2009). The psychology of success is realized through asset-building efforts that are critical to positive youth development.

The America's Promise Alliance (2009) summarizes the assets into these *Five Promises*. While the items might seem obvious, it is important to remember that many children do not have these assets in their lives:

- Caring adults.
- Safe places.
- A healthy start and healthy development.
- An effective education.
- Opportunities to help others through service.

The Search Institute has done extensive research on the personal and environmental factors that make children and youth resilient to negative life circumstances. They have identified *40 Developmental Assets* that provide students with the family, school, and community resources, opportunities, and personal skills they need to grow into intelligent, mentally and physically healthy adults.

To find out how well these needs were being met, in 2002 the Institute administered the *Search Institute Profiles of Student Life: Attitudes and Behaviors* survey to approximately 150,000 children in grades 6–12 in 202 communities across the country. In an ideal world, all students would report having each of the 40 developmental assets in their lives, but this was not the case. Looking at some of the individual assets, 37 percent said they had a *caring neighborhood*, 52 percent felt a *bonding to school,* and just 27 percent said they had *adult role models* (How Many Youth Experience Each Asset? 2002).

DEVELOPING A SAFE SCHOOL CLIMATE PLAN

Comprehensive safe school climate efforts build assets and are all-inclusive, employing a four-stage plan of prevention, early intervention, late intervention, and post-incident response to cover all aspects of the cycle of violence (Figure 6.1). Members use their intra- and interpersonal skills to regularly re-evaluate the school's violence prevention and response efforts. This monitoring lets us know when we are backsliding in our objectives, getting complacent, or have gaps in our efforts.

Violence exists on a continuum and so does an effective comprehensive school safety plan. An effective plan addresses all levels of violence and emphasizes respect as the foundation for all interactions. As districts and schools put together their plans, the violence continuum provides them with a common foundation for assessing school climate and breaches in safety and security. This is the rational for doing the violence continuum activity as the first step of any planning.

The most important distinguishing feature of the plan is starting early and taking it seriously. Wise districts focus their efforts on positive youth development and the psychology of success in the prevention and early intervention stages, where efforts are the most cost effective and can do the most good for the most members. A psychology of success can improve a poor school climate and elevate an already positive school climate to an even higher level.

PREVENTION

Safe Schools Have a Plan For

EARLY INTERVENTION

POST-INCIDENT RESPONSE

LATE INTERVENTION

Figure 6.1.

STAGE 1: PREVENTION

Prevention begins with assessment of the *physical safety* of the school buildings and campus to identify and correct breaches in security using a more formal version of the audit presented at the beginning of the chapter. Safety audits are available on the Internet for schools to use as walk-around checklists. Audits look for things such as unlocked and unmonitored entrances, procedures for visitors to sign in, if there is sufficient outdoor lighting around the school perimeter and in parking lots, how behavior on school buses is supervised, where tardy students are told to report, if the playground is fenced and monitored by adults when children are present, and whether the school practices emergency drills.

As an elementary school principal, my students were once evacuated because of a bomb scare, likely a Halloween prank, and had to walk to an alternate shelter. We discovered it was difficult to see and hear the members of the school safety team directing our five hundred students away from traffic. In our post-incident debriefing we decided to purchase bright yellow reflective safety vests with loud whistles.

47%
Schools that reported they had drills for a school shooting.
(Bradshawet al. 2010)

DEVELOPING STANDARDS FOR CONDUCT

With security breaches in the physical plant addressed, we move on to the human component of violence prevention. What does this look like in a school? It looks a lot like a school climate plan that educates for good moral character and acceptance of diversity. Developmental assets are built through healthy school partnerships with parents and instruction is relevant and motivating. We respect students' need for power and give them a chance to make decisions about what goes on in their classroom and school.

Prevention provides asset building through conflict resolution training, cross-grade buddy systems, anti-bullying training, and school and community service projects. It takes the form of a unifying code of conduct that describes how we should treat each other. Rules are discussed and developed by adults and students. Non-instructional settings such as lunch, recess, bathrooms, waiting to enter before school, waiting for the bus to go home, and riding on the school bus are well supervised and the same rules and expectations are applied everywhere. The school recognizes that misbehavior is common during transition times and they actively work to improve the climate of each of these environments using volunteers or staff.

This is the school code of conduct my students and their K–5 teachers created and sent home to families:

We come to school to learn about our world.
We are responsible for:
• *Our choices, our learning, and our environment.*
• *Treating others with kindness and respect.*
• *Helping and sharing.*
• *Working together.*
We look out for each other!

ESTABLISHING THE CLASSROOM CLIMATE

The words of the code of conduct translate into behavior. In classrooms, prevention looks like respect for others, where meanness, putdowns, name-calling, and intolerance are not allowed by students, or by adults. Prevention efforts are tailored to meet the unique needs of the school, grade level, and the particular class and students. Teachers employ effective teaching strategies that stress collaboration in place of competition. Partnering, cooperative learning, class meetings, teamwork, and personally relevant learning experiences put schools on track to creating an exciting, caring learning community that respects differences.

The goals of prevention are to create positive respectful adult-student, student-student, and adult-adult relationships and provide an education that is rich with character-building challenges. Pro-social skills lead to ethical behavior and rewarding relationships. Children can be actively taught these positive skills and held to high, developmentally appropriate expectations for behavior. They learn the language of cooperation and conflict resolution, the self-control necessary to express themselves peacefully, and how to make their needs known without resorting to violence. Students whose self-preservation instincts tell them to get what they want through violence are taught strategies to control their anger.

During this stage we teach students about bullying and harassment, the roles students play when bullying happens, ways to protect themselves from real life and cyber bullying, and what to do if they are bullied or witness bullying. One of the most important messages we send to our students is that if they are being bullied or harassed it is not their fault, and they do not have to suffer. We make sure they know there are adults in the school who care about and will help them. Teachers at every grade level express and show commitment to the students, cognizant that the older children get, the more aware they are of any unfairness, insincerity, or hypocrisy in the system, and the more intractable their disappointment in adults. Children and young people need to be able to count on us to be consistent and caring resources in their lives.

Now we add a positive, dignity-preserving discipline approach that is modeled and practiced by classroom teachers, building principals, and staff. This approach emphasizes accepting responsibility, problem solving, making restitution, and learning new behaviors to replace the old. The school principal leads this effort and applies non-violent, character building principles to her interactions with students. Both teachers and administrators willingly invest extra time to help students who are having problems.

When teachers look closely at themselves, they can have a significant effect on school climate. We can immediately improve the climate by not doing the disrespectful, ineffective, hurtful practices we might be in the habit of doing, including yelling at students and shaming or embarrassing them in front of their peers.

The climate improves drastically when teachers move from an *Assertive Discipline* approach (i.e., writing a student's name on the board and adding check marks for each additional offense) to one of "discipline with dignity." The *Privacy—Eye Contact—Proximity* (P.E.P.) approach advises adults to get physically close to the student (but not in their personal space), with as much privacy as possible (or is wise), to speak quietly and calmly with confidence, and to look the child in the eye (with sensitivity to cultural norms) (Mendler 1992, 41). This low-key intervention is an appropriate time to ask three simple "w" questions: What were you doing? Why is that behavior a problem? What are you going to do now instead?

HURTFUL BEHAVIOR IS ABNORMAL

Comprehensive plans are careful to intentionally celebrate the positive at the same time they remediate the negative. Research finds students' perceptions of risky and hurtful behavior, what they think are the norms in their school, are often inaccurate. The discrepancies are sizable between perceived norms and actual norms. Middle school students think a greater percentage of their peers bully others and think it is okay to bully, tease, and make fun of others than is actually the case. Students who are insecure or feel alienated are more likely to believe negative behavior is the norm. They think they need to behave this way themselves to gain respect and status. Such misconceptions are the strongest predictors of a child's level of vulnerability and the use of offensive, and self-protective behavior (Perkins and Craig n.d.).

Schools can dispel the myths about peer behavior by advertising the positive norms that are often overshadowed by our focus on the negative. A positive norms approach is compatible with asset-building approaches that focus on building strengths rather than targeting perceived weaknesses. Perkins and Craig report that, "Evidence has shown youth responding to these initiatives with more realistic perceptions of peers, problem behavior decreasing, and the norm of positive behavior growing stronger in the population." Students discover they do or can fit into the mainstream—the healthy mainstream.

Schools can conduct a poll or student attitude and behavior survey, or use an anonymous online questionnaire to find out what students believe about violence. Questions should concentrate on the subtle and middle span of the violence continuum, making sure to include examples of relational aggression. Ask students how strongly they agree or disagree with statements such as:

• Students should not make fun of others because of how they look.
• Name-calling and teasing are hurtful.
• It is not okay to spread rumors about someone.
• If someone bullies you or you see someone being bullied, you should tell an adult.
• Cyber-bullying is okay because no one can see you.

The statistics collected can then be used to affirm the positive attitudes and behavior of the students in our school. For example, a poster could highlight the following messages:

• 9 out of 10 McKinley MS students think it is not okay to make fun of someone for how they look.
• 80 percent of McKinley MS students think students should report bullying to an adult.

In the response to the perennial argument that "everyone does it," publicizing these positive peer group attitudes normalizes pro-social, non-violent behavior. Hang up posters of these norms and send copies home to parents. Get the word out any way you can.

The positive youth norms approach might not produce dramatic results in cases of entrenched anti-social systems such as hate groups, gang culture, and violent neighborhoods where targeted law enforcement interventions are necessary. But it can still provide a peer group for students of good character who want to do well in school and are trying to resist the negative influences around them. Students who once felt they did not belong now have an instant positive peer group. Students who are on the fence or who are already violent, and the victims of violence get the message that these things are not okay or necessary to fit in. It also identifies their school as a place where positive norms are valued and the assets that provide support and build resilience are practiced.

Normalizing positive behavior does not change the reality that there are students who are perpetrators and victims of hurtful behaviors. If 80 percent of our students feel it is not okay to use racial and ethnic slurs, we still have to deal with the 20 percent who do think it is okay (Perkins and Craig 2009). However, this approach does succeed in labeling this behavior as *abnormal*: out of the norm.

There is a strong benefit to framing school climate efforts in a positive way. School staff will get behind something that is worded in the affirmative, whereas they might balk at or dispute norms that criticize the school. They would not want negative information to be used to characterize their school as a place where bullying is rampant or students are afraid to walk the halls. We can be honest and work to improve the school climate, while at the same time having empathy for people who might feel they are being criticized.

INTENTIONALLY CREATING A POSITIVE NORM

Vivian Gussin Paley, former kindergarten teacher and researcher at the University of Chicago Laboratory School, witnessed the unjust structure of *haves* and *have nots* as it developed in the classes she taught, and watched it become more and more entrenched as the children moved through school. Expressed in her classic book, *You Can't Say You Can't Play,* Paley's realization is a simple and disturbing one: "Certain children will have the right to limit the social experiences of their classmates . . . long after hitting and name-calling have been outlawed by the teachers, a more damaging phenomenon is allowed to take root, spreading like a weed from grade to grade" (Paley 1992, 3).

She did something about the rise of dominant personalities by making a new classroom rule: You can't say you can't play. Her book chronicles her experiences trying to change the social climate and culture of her school. She started with changes in her classroom and eventually changed the culture of the school. Her interventions gave a voice to the majority of children who act in positive, kind ways—the norm. They rejected the negative attention-seeking behavior of the few who chose to be hurtful and exclude others, behavior that taints the climate for everyone else in the classroom.

Teaching students about the roles they choose to play in bullying and other violence creates awareness where children can see how their unthinking behavior influences the safety and peaceful enjoyment of others. This empowers them to believe they can make a positive difference in their world. They know what is right and take a stand, refusing to participate in or allow hurtful things to happen.

Prevention efforts like these connect the expanded New Golden Rule of Empathy with the violence continuum and replace common forms of subtle violence with peaceful skills and attitudes. We can imagine the impact on our children if these prevention messages were a part of their educational experience for six hours per day, five days per week, for all thirteen of their formative years. Imagine the impact on the climate and security of our schools and the adults we would send out into the world. Thanks to asset-building prevention efforts we would never again feel that we do not have the power to keep our schools safe or to raise good people.

Prevention efforts target the whole school community and include:

The Foundation:

- Understanding that violence occurs along a continuum.
- Mutually respectful and caring relationships among student, parents, and staff.
- Education and involvement of all school staff in school climate efforts.
- Teachers who do not use violence with students, parents, or colleagues.
- Parental involvement and education.
- Developmental asset building.
- Alcohol and illegal drug use education.
- Classroom and school codes of conduct that are worded positively and made with student input.
- The message that it is not the child's fault if he is bullied, and that adults will intervene to protect him.
- Committing to making respect for diversity an integral part of the curriculum and everyday school life.

Actions:

- Sharing power.
- Teaching and modeling pro-social skills.
- Making sure every child is a proficient reader by third grade and continues to make good progress toward graduation.
- Using engaging curriculum materials and instructional approaches that students find relevant, motivating, and fun.
- Teaching about bullying behavior and learning the roles students play in bullying, and teaching defender/ally behavior.
- Designing school and classroom activities and projects that require collaboration and cooperation, rather than competition that separates students into winners and losers, haves and have-nots.
- Treating students with dignity while holding them accountable for their behavior.
- Teaching conflict resolution and peer mediation skills.
- Conducting school safety, security, and climate audits.
- Offering before and after-school programs.
- Providing adult mentors and tutors who are positive role models.

STAGE 2: EARLY INTERVENTION

With effective violence prevention efforts in place, the next part of the safe school climate plan addresses those children who are not internalizing and applying the prevention messages to their lives. Students who lash out violently or who seem to relish hurting others frustrate, shock, and scare us. They do not learn (internalize for use in the future) from our efforts to teach them better ways of being, nor do they seem to learn from practice or experience. They may show a lack of empathy and remorse and exhibit signs of covert aggression—doing negative things in an underhanded way and denying culpability for their behavior if caught in the act.

In early intervention we take a serious and sometimes unsettling look at who our children are and what they are telling us about themselves and the world in which they live. At these times teachers, administrators, and most especially parents have to admit we do not have all the answers and that some children can be challenging to reach. The staff of a safe school does not acquiesce and let negative behavior continue, nor does it give up on helping these children no matter how challenging it may be.

160,000
Students who go home early on any given
day for fear of being bullied.
(CDC 2008)

What do early interventions look like in a school? They range from individual anger-management training to mentoring and counseling and to support groups designed to teach coping skills. Positive school norms efforts can sway children who have one foot on the side of trouble to step back and join the majority of their well-behaved peers. Early intervention makes sure students have trusted adults they can talk to and who check in on them regularly, and know that their concerns are taken seriously and addressed. Students, including those who are the source of misbehavior, are made to feel safe and not alone. They also experience a team approach that includes teachers, specialists, and their parents or guardians. Most students respond well to these early intervention efforts and a strong student support system can be the deciding factor in the child's future.

Tyler Lee Long was a seventeen year old high school junior with Asperger's Syndrome. He was also harassed and hounded relentlessly by classmates until one day in October 2009 he committed "bullycide." He hung himself in his bedroom closet.

This tragedy could have been averted if Tyler had received help and adult intervention to stop the harassment. He could have benefited from these four components of an effective anti-bullying strategy that catch inappropriate behavior early on and prevent it from happening again:

1. Adults intervene when they witness violence of all levels.
2. Teachers and parents prepare students to stick up for those being targeted.
3. Consequences are consistent and enforcement fair.
4. There is continuous anti-bullying education for all members of the school community. (Ollove 2010)

Special needs students, such as Tyler, may require individual instruction on how to resist being bullied and to learn how to avoid bullying others. Such instruction is a critical component of an IEP or 504 Plan. A functional behavior assessment is used to define specific strengths, challenges, and goals for behavior. The plan then offers specific recommendations for how school staff should react to and redirect the child if she misbehaves. An IEP or 504 Plan behavior plan is critical information and federal law requires it must be implemented in any classroom or in any other school-related venue where the child spends part of her time. The plans are confidential and on a need to know basis teachers and aides who interact with the child have a right to and should read their students' plans. This ensures the staff is prepared with the proper approach to respond to verbal or physical acting out, and with strategies to prevent students from becoming a target.

6.5 million
The number of children and youth ages 3–21 receiving special education services in 2008–09, about 13 percent of all public school enrollment. (Condition of Education Overview 2011)

UNCOVERING COVERT AGGRESSION

What about the covert aggression of a child who hurts and dominates others, who seems to act without conscience or remorse? He may appear to be a nice kid on the outside, when he actually not only enjoys his power to bully and manipulate, it is his motivating drive. This hidden aggression usually occurs on the subtle end to the midpoint of the violence continuum.

These children are skilled at hiding their intentions and behavior. Eventually, as other children report incidents and teachers use their keen powers of observation, they begin to notice something is not right. There is a pattern to the complaints and when confronted with the problem the child expresses no remorse for the misbehavior and often tries to shift the blame to others.

What does covert aggression look like? It looks like meanness, intentional harm done in a sneaky way. Two examples come to mind from my experience as an elementary school principal. One involved an intermediate grade girl who had temporarily moved away with her family with the intention of returning to the school. Many months into her absence a few students in her grade finally confided to a teacher they trusted that this child was harassing a female classmate. We came to find out that she had been writing shockingly mean-spirited, aggressive letters to her friends back home, telling them to ostracize the targeted girl, and even said that she was going to kill her when she returned.

From thousands of miles away she manipulated and controlled a group of her peers and turned them into aggressors and bullies. They allowed themselves to be her pawns. The ringleader was at the top of the social heap, a position of great power, and she used it to make life miserable for another child. It was both female relational and covert aggression.

The child's behavior and her outward persona did not match. She seemed to be an ideal student, bright, hard working, and polite. No one would have guessed what she was up to under the radar. Her parents were shocked to discover this behavior, but rationalized it was just pre-teen girl stuff and that she was missing home. We advised them that this was not typical and that their daughter's hurtful behavior needed to be taken seriously and addressed.

Another case involved a second grade boy whom I met when his grandfather died. He was acting up in school so the teacher, thinking he was upset about the loss, asked me to sit down with him. We sat in my office talking about his grandfather and how he felt about losing him. He described what happened in detail and with something I thought interesting—a level of emotional detachment, like a reporter giving a news report. He was chipper, smiling, and very verbal. He was polite and personable, and appeared to be enjoying my undivided attention. He seemed happy when he left my office to return to his classroom, which left me unsettled rather than comforted.

I soon had regular interactions with this child due to a pattern of hurtful behavior and non-compliance. He denied responsibility when caught misbehaving in the boy's bathroom taunting a child with special needs. He was also involved in other anti-social behaviors, but this one boy in particular had become the target of his aggression.

As the classroom teacher, school social worker, school psychologist, his parents and I worked with the child, we became aware that he did not seem to care that he hurt someone. He continued to act in covertly and sometimes overtly aggressive ways, but we were now aware of his personality and were not fooled. We asked his parents for some effective approaches to try. They understood our concerns but did not have many suggestions to offer; they were as frustrated as we were. They took him for outside counseling, and he met with the school social worker during the school day. He usually behaved well in front of adults but was still often in the center of some bullying incident.

When I left the school three years later, he was one of the children I was most worried about. I knew the social worker would speak with the middle school team to prepare them for his arrival. This was not to prejudice the teachers and principal before they met the child, but rather was part of an ongoing early intervention effort to avert potential problems and continue his support services. The more time spent on early interventions the better the chance that children can learn and be turned around—or at least monitored closely.

Students who exhibit anti- and asocial behavior, who have an oppositional defiant or conduct disorder require mental health interventions the school cannot typically provide. A team of school personnel, parents, and mental health professionals best serves the child and protects other students from his destructive behavior.

Early intervention efforts target those students not responsive to prevention efforts that need individual attention through:

- Anger-management training.
- Counseling in or out of school.
- Support groups for specific needs.
- Developmental asset development.
- Family involvement and education.
- School support/child study team coordination and assessment.
- Peer mediation and conflict resolution.
- Adult mentoring.
- Behavior plans.
- Staff training to recognize and respond to warning signs.

STAGE 3: LATE INTERVENTION

We know that even our best attempts at prevention and early intervention may not ward off all violent incidents, so we have a late intervention plan poised to respond to a student crisis or other emergency. This is where we put our crisis response team, building evacuation plan, and partnerships with law enforcement agencies into action. Thorough crisis management planning and practice is essential to respond to the most serious and potentially deadly level of violent behavior seen in schools.

In a safe school, where physical safety and security of each member of the school community are the highest priority, school teachers and other staff are skilled observers of students. They know what to look for and how to intervene early and safely. A critical component and one missing in many educational settings is crisis de-escalation training for staff, where they are taught how to recognize the signs of impending trouble and respond in a way that makes the situation better instead of worse. Crisis response efforts deserve and require the same level of attention and seriousness given to the age-old practice of fire drills. These skills can diffuse a potentially explosive situation and keep students and staff from being hurt.

Early warning signs are not definitive and absolute, but there are likely to be clues alerting us that a child might need help. *Early Warning, Timely Response: A Guide to Safe Schools* (2001) cautions us not to unfairly label students "potentially violent" because they fit a stereotype. With that said school personnel should be aware of the early warning signs and to intervene when they see indicators that a child may be on the verge of acting violently toward himself or others:

- Serious physical fighting with peers or family members.
- Severe destruction of property.
- Severe rage for seemingly minor reasons.
- Detailed threats of lethal violence.
- Possession and/or use of firearms and other weapons.
- Self-injurious behaviors or threats of suicide.

DE-ESCALATING PROBLEM BEHAVIOR

The key in de-escalating problem behavior is to know what to do. In "Managing Escalating Behavior" (n.d.) the U.S. Department of Education Center for Positive Behavioral Prevention and Support advises that crisis intervention training helps adults assess where the student is on a continuum of emotional states—calm, trigger, agitation, acceleration, peak, de-escalation, or recovery—so they can respond appropriately and bring the student back to calm or into recovery as soon as possible.

The South Carolina Department of Education participated in non-violent crises intervention training from the Crisis Prevention Institute (CPI). Mike Paget, coordinator for the state initiative, explained why it is important to be prepared: "In any group of students, you will have a range of kids, including some whose background may cause them to be volatile and reactive. . . . We have seen scary situations in which potential violence has been defused and problems avoided thanks to these techniques—the individuals are shown respect and non-verbal cues that are non-threatening or non-provoking to them." South Carolina established a network of over 100 teacher trainers throughout the state and reports success in:

- Reducing the frequency and severity of disruptive or dangerous situations.
- Increasing employee confidence and morale.

- Fostering a culture of respect and safety in schools.
- Preserving dignity as well as safety for adults and students (Case Study: South Carolina Dept. of Education n.d.).

Aggression can be reactive or predatory. Reactive aggression is a defensive response to being or feeling threatened, where people respond automatically to a threat with primal fight or flight self-preservation responses. Predatory aggression is an offensive action initiated to threaten or attack another person. De-escalation strategies work with both types of aggression and give school personnel confidence that they will do the right thing in an emergency. Without such training, it is a hit or miss situation that is dependent on the individual teacher. For adults who are not accustomed to dealing with challenging students or who never faced a crisis before, it is common to react on their own anxieties and respond in ways that unintentionally make the situation worse. We could all benefit from the calming techniques of de-escalation training when trying to defuse a tense situation or violent outburst.

The basic principle of a non-violent crisis intervention program, also described as a therapeutic intervention, is to assess the emotional level of the agitated student. When we respond we keep our voice and energy a level below that of the student, we position ourselves so the student has an escape route (do not stand between the student and the exit), and let the student talk instead of doing a lot of talking and questioning. It is critical to stay out of the student's personal space—a cultural comfort zone of about three feet for Americans. If a student is already upset, it is not helpful to have someone's face in his.

Arguing with someone who is upset or irrational is perceived as threatening and, not only does it not help, it can make the situation worse. In our personal lives when we are upset and ready to react, we might tell ourselves to sleep on it before responding and to see how we feel in the morning when we are more rational. This cooling off period brings us back from an emotional to rational state of mind and prevents us from doing something we will be sorry about. The same is true of students who act out. While the child is upset, do not ask him why he did something or chastise him about what he did wrong. Our primary goal in this situation is to return him to a calm state. Then it is time to deal with the problem behavior itself.

Non-violent crisis intervention has another dimension, one that teaches the use of safe physical restraint techniques to keep a student who is acting out from hurting herself or someone else. These techniques are for protection only, not a way of pursuing or subduing a perpetrator. That is left to law enforcement.

Non-violent crisis intervention is one of the most important trainings school staff can receive. The knowledge and skills you learn serve you every day in the classroom as well as in personal and work relationships. These skills give people confidence that they will respond in the most constructive way for the situation and that they can be the difference between an incident and a tragedy.

Late intervention efforts target those committing an overt act and include:

- Activation of the crisis response plan.
- De-escalation strategies.
- Non-violent crisis intervention.
- Isolation from other students.
- Removal from the classroom or school.
- Involvement of law enforcement.
- Media communication to parents and the students.

STAGE 4: POST-INCIDENT RESPONSE

Rounding out the safe school climate cycle is post-incident response for those times when a violent episode could not be avoided. During this phase we offer post-incident counseling to those who need it, critique events leading up to and during the crisis, and use the information to improve prevention, early and late intervention, and response efforts. In this phase we sit down as a team, including a law enforcement officer if appropriate, and take a serious look at the crisis we just experienced. Information is gathered and assessed so we can sort out what went well and what we need to do better in the future. We congratulate ourselves for appropriate responses and identify weaknesses in our efforts, looking for signs of potential violence we might have missed. We modify our prevention, early intervention, and late intervention efforts with a pledge to not miss the signs the next time.

Post-incident response efforts target everyone affected and include:

- Incident debriefing with staff and law enforcement.
- Media communication.
- Counseling services.
- Follow-up with the student body and communication with the parents of students.
- Debriefing meeting with the student(s) involved and meting out of consequences.
- A superintendent's hearing.

- Alternative student placement.
- Critique and revision of the crisis response plan.
- Identification of additional prevention and early intervention efforts needed.
- Implementation of new ideas.
- Community-building efforts to help heal the school climate.

Equations That Add Up
Violence Continuum + Pro-social skills = Prevention

Chapter 7

How Do We Intentionally Teach Our Children to Be Non-Violent?

But if you ask what is good of education in general, the answer is easy: that education makes good men, and that good men act nobly.

—Plato

Tolerance, empathy, and compassion are critical elements of a non-violent learning environment and the heart of the prevention efforts we just outlined. The foundation of a safe school is created when teachers and students share a common understanding of violence, and when all aspects of school life teach, reinforce, and expect pro-social behavior.

Once students understand the concept of violence as a spectrum of behaviors from subtle to obvious, we can work on developing specific skills and attitudes. Below are three ways of approaching conflict, paired with their comparable cycle level (Beckman 2011).

- Peacekeeping—control overt behavior (Late intervention)
- Peacemaking—respond with focus to resolve the conflict (Early intervention)
- Peace-building—develop long term systems that "de-normalize violence" and build and "rebuild social relationships" (Prevention)

This model parallels the school safety cycle and is helpful in making sure our efforts give us the outcome we want. A successful comprehensive safe school climate effort goes beyond peacekeeping (intervention) to the prevention realm of peace building, where children are taught and given the opportunity to practice how to use peaceful choices and attitudes. We learn how to build peace when we:

- Hold regular class meetings.
- Have students participate in the development of class rules and codes of conduct.
- Teach mediation of problems to develop pro-social skills and attitudes.
- Offer opportunities to cooperate and work together to contribute to the school and to community.
- Use service projects to help students connect with others and to feel they belong, are appreciated, and have something constructive to offer.
- Listen to students' concerns about their emotional and physical safety and take swift, thoughtful action.
- Provide alternative avenues for students to resolve conflicts peacefully.
- Consider the existing academic curriculum and teaching practices to be part of the school's prevention efforts and concentrate on the underlying concepts of social justice.
- Intentionally elevate our efforts to raise good people and reduce violence to a high level of consciousness.
- Intervene early when prevention efforts are unsuccessful.
- Integrate all violence prevention efforts into the climate and eventually the culture of the school as a way of *being* rather than something to do.

MOTIVATED FROM WITHIN

Fostering long-lasting high personal standards for behavior requires a positive approach to discipline that teaches responsibility (intrinsic motivation) rather than expects obedience (extrinsic motivation). We live by the belief that people are more likely to follow guidelines for behavior (rules) that they have explored, understand, had a role in developing, and view as fair. The school, classroom, and home are the most natural and logical places to give children an active role in defining what it means to be part of a healthy, well-functioning community. This includes defining the rights and responsibilities shared by all members of the group.

In *Discipline with Dignity,* Curwin and Mendler (1998) underscore the importance of a *responsibility model* of classroom management over the traditional *obedience model.* The obedience model sends the message that students must follow the rules that adults impose without question regardless of the students' ideas of right and wrong, special needs or circumstances, instincts and experiences, or values. The message from adults is, "You must behave in a certain way because I have the power, and I tell you to do it."

This approach loses sight of the fact that the child is in school to learn and fails to consider context. And children are often shamed by this bullying discipline method. While the concept of obedience might tempt us with its promise of order and a return to the submissive compliance of previous generations, it does not advance our goal to establish a positive school climate and grow thinking human beings.

Obedience develops behavior motivated by an external *locus of control* rather than an internal conscience. When a student's primary goal is to avoid being caught, this can motivate him to hide or lie about his behavior. If he is caught, he may blame it on someone else or try to get even with the oppressor. For those students with the most serious emotional and behavior issues it may trigger emotional withdrawal or increase acting out. This creates an adversarial and disrespectful environment that damages the single most important factor for a safe and effective school climate: positive relationships among members.

Obedience may offer teachers or parents:

- The power of an absolute authority.
- A sense that they have the power and control over their children.
- A predetermined comprehensive list of rules and matching punishments.
- Some hope of keeping students "in line."
- And the most alluring of all—compliance.

But a focus on obedience also leads to children who:

- Lack emotional maturity and self-discipline.
- Are not able to think critically or problem solve and make decisions.
- Feel powerless and frustrated.
- Withdraw or "act out."
- Blame others for their behavior.
- Engage in power struggles.
- And the last thing we want to promote: act in aggressive ways (covertly and overtly).

Compare this to another message that can be communicated to students: We respect you as an individual with basic needs and hopes, and we believe you have or can develop the skills to make constructive choices. We understand the context of your life and will hold you to a high standard while we guide you to be successful.

Such a climate, based on *rights and responsibilities,* offers teachers:

- Healthy relationships with students.
- Satisfying interactions and more time to teach.

- Less frustration and more success with handling misbehavior.
- A redefinition of their role from warden to mentor.
- A sharing of power.
- Steady progress toward accomplishing meaningful goals.
- The chance to take discipline off the top of their list of concerns.

And it leads to students and eventually to citizens who:

- Are intrinsically motivated.
- Have a sense of right and wrong.
- Are critical and creative problem-solvers who make healthy choices.
- Work toward the good of the community.
- Are not afraid to take the emotional and intellectual risks needed to learn.
- Recognize and respect the rights of others.
- Act ethically.
- Stand up for what they believe is right.
- Take responsibility and fix any messes they make.

The rights and responsibilities approach asks students to consider how they should behave in the classroom and school in order for everyone to get along and have an opportunity to learn. We can ask them to describe the perfect classroom and use their ideas as the foundation of our safe school climate efforts. Students then see the rationale behind behavior guidelines and understand the cause and effect of their actions.

When the code of conduct or a rule is broken, we keep the focus on the child's internal locus of control and remember that we are there to teach. We want them to develop an internal guidance system, not to behave well just because they are being watched. We can ask them to apply the New Golden Rule of Empathy to situations and use a written behavior plan that teaches problem solving to help them move along a path that builds character. Such a plan might include the following questions:

1. What behavior got you here?
2. Why was that behavior a problem?
3. What could you choose to do instead next time?
4. How will you make amends for your behavior now?

THE ROLES STUDENTS PLAY IN BULLYING

Through role-playing we explore the positions students play in school violence as a victim (target), perpetrator and co-perpetrator, ally (defender), bystander, audience, and cheerleader. Role-playing exposes students to the viewpoints of all players in an incident, creates empathy for the victim, builds a feeling of efficacy, and might be the catalyst for a child's self-realization that he is bullying others.

We teach skills to resist being a target of bullying and encourage students to be positive role models. StopBullying.gov is a website that provides information from various federal agencies on how to prevent or stop bullying. It tells us that basic peacemaking behavior comes from taking a stand to not join in bullying, walking away when it happens, and befriending the person being bullied. It advises that—*if* the bystander feels it is safe—he or she take on the role of ally or defender by firmly telling the perpetrator one of the following: "Stop it," "Don't call him that," or "What you are saying (doing) is mean."

It would be nice to have one set approach to stop bullies in their tracks, but life is more complicated than that, and each interaction is influenced by specific circumstances and the nature of those involved. Bullies are often physically and mentally strong, act in groups, and have a sense of entitlement that is resistant to correction. Standing up to them does not always work and the target or defender can get hurt in the process.

An adult who is told about bullying may not choose to step in right away. To achieve the best outcome, certain factors must be considered such as how long the bullying has been going on, whether it is increasing in frequency or seriousness, if it is physical, qualifies as harassment, and what attempts the target has made to try to stop it. Depending on the specifics of the situation, a parent, counselor, or teacher might coach the child on ways to stand up to the bully, help him rehearse the exact things to say, and teach him how to assess danger and get away to seek immediate help when necessary. Practical life skills like these teach children how to convey confidence, show resistance, and apply measures to avoid or handle dangerous situations.

These strategies do not put the blame or responsibility for the misbehavior of the perpetrator on the target and do not mean we leave victims to fend for themselves. Adult guidance is necessary throughout this process, as it might take a few different approaches by the student to achieve success—and some interventions might backfire only to make the situation worse. By keeping communication open with the child, an adult will be aware of what is going on and can be prepared to step in to provide direct intervention if necessary; the victim is never left to handle it on his own. And if they are being bullied or harassed, they need to tell the perpetrator to stop.

The roles students play in cyberbullying are similar to face-to-face bullying, but pose new challenges when it comes to free speech and electronic media. The courts have not kept up with the technology. It is critical that schools use legal advice when they develop written rules that specifically address the Internet, cyberbullying, and use of electronic media at school.

Communications posted, texted, or emailed at school come under the school guidelines for behavior but first amendment issues complicate the issue.

Dr. Kathleen Conn, assistant professor in education at Neumann University and an expert on cyberbullying, says that schools are in a difficult position. School officials "want to step in, but their collective hands have been slapped by the courts so many times that they are reluctant" (Davis 2011). It appears schools and law enforcement cannot interfere with the first amendment right to free speech even if what is said is hurtful, but they can intervene if there is a school nexus—a direct connection—that interferes with students' ability to learn or causes substantial harm, such as when threats are made, there is coercion, obscene or harassing text messages, harassment or stalking, a possible hate or bias crime, if a sexually explicit picture is created or sent, or a picture was taken of someone in private. (Cyberbullying or Cyberthreat Situation Review Process 2005).

The New York Center for School Safety offers Cyber Safety: Ten Tips (n.d.), a checklist for students that cautions them not to use screen names that reveal personal information, to keep passwords private, and not to send messages when they are angry (n.d.).

CyberBullying: What Kids, Teens, and Adults Can Do (n.d.) advises we teach students strategies to avoid being a victim of cyber-bullying, including the following:

- Think about what you post.
- Do not take part in or cheer on bullying.
- Use privacy settings.
- Do not respond to cyber-bullying.

Children should also be taught what to do if they are a victim of cyberbullying, including:

- Tell someone you trust.
- Keep evidence of cyberbullying.
- Block the offender.
- Report it to school.
- Ask for help.

SOCIAL-EMOTIONAL LEARNING AT CLASS MEETINGS

Mistreatment of each other would not come up as an issue if we were able to successfully teach students to be thoughtful, caring people starting at a young age. Research has identified five common elements of effective character education and other social-emotional initiatives. Such initiatives focus on developing the following:

- Positive social skills.
- Empathy.
- Self-management.
- Decision-making skills.
- How to listen to and communicate with others. (Boccanfuso and Kuhfeld 2011, 6)

A class meeting is a process that includes all five elements. *Positive Discipline* by Jane Nelsen (2006) and *Developing Capable Young People* by H. Stephen Glenn (1985) advanced the concept of regular, structured classroom meetings as a means of teaching critical pro-social skills. The meetings provide students with the opportunity to express appreciation to others, solve problems, practice communication skills, celebrate successes, and plan activities.

Each class meeting begins with students sitting in a circle so everyone can see each other. Then, one-by-one around the circle, students recognize and thank others for specific acts of kindness and support. Generic praise such as "she was nice to me" is not accepted. Students are encouraged to thank others for specific actions such as, "I want to thank Johnny for helping me pick up the crayons." The class meeting continues with agenda items suggested beforehand by students or the teacher, usually problems or concerns that need resolution. The owner of the problem leads the discussion and solicits ideas from classmates. As the group explores real life issues in a thoughtful way, students practice expressing concerns calmly, listening respectfully and patiently to the ideas of others, and exploring constructive ways to resolve problems. They experience the power of a team effort and learn how it feels to be part of a working, supportive community, one where people listen to you. Class meetings give every child a voice.

Class meetings quickly become a treasured part of classroom life, so much so that students may choose to pass up a scheduled recess to fit in a meeting. The class meeting process teaches us to tolerate ambiguity—there may be more than one right solution to a problem—and that insightful ideas often come from those we least expect.

Children become engaged when we validate and attend to real-life issues that are important to them. Engaged children pay attention, internalize, and grow from the experience. This attention and practice over years of schooling teaches them the skills and attitudes that help them become good people.

Class meetings give students at any grade level, including kindergarten, a chance to practice these specific pro-social skills:

- Listening respectfully when others speak.
- Brainstorming ideas.
- Giving and receiving compliments.
- Dealing honestly with problems.
- Problem-solving with others.
- Accepting different speaking styles and ways of thinking.
- Considering the point of view of others.
- Reflecting the mood of others.
- Feeling and showing empathy.
- Giving positive feedback.
- Taking turns.
- Including each person in the process.
- Respecting the rights of individuals and the group.
- Compromising to reach an agreement.
- Making and keeping agreements.

Class meetings also give students a chance to practice verbal skills, including:

- Expressing appreciation to others.
- Asking for help.
- Clearly articulating a need or concern.
- Expressing feelings.
- Asking questions to clarify.
- Offering solutions.
- Staying on topic.
- Choosing wording that is respectful and helpful.

The ABCs of Problem Solving

✓ Ask about and identify each person's needs.

✓ Brainstorm possible solutions that meet common needs.

✓ Commit to solutions that meet common needs.

RESOLVING CONFLICTS PEACEFULLY

Schools bring together students that are diverse in culture, socio-economic status, ambitions, maturity, and values. These students are often in close physical proximity in overcrowded classrooms, halls, cafeterias, school buses, and locker rooms where it is easy to unintentionally violate someone else's personal space. They are also under tremendous academic and social pressures that escalate as they navigate adolescence and near graduation. And all along the way, the quest for social status and recognition is a powerful driving force. Is it any surprise that school can be a hotbed for intense interactions and disagreements?

One solution to these inevitable conflicts is mediation. Mediation and conflict resolution are not the same as crisis intervention or emergency response plans. They take place at different points in the safe schools cycle. Mediation is a basic process of problem solving using a neutral third party (the mediator) to help resolve the daily conflicts that are a part of life. Through teacher and parent modeling students can learn, beginning in the early elementary years, to use these simple problem-solving steps of mediation to settle disagreements:

Step 1: Set ground rules

- Both parties promise to be honest and to work toward a solution.
- They also promise to listen to each other without interrupting.

Step 2: Explore perspectives

- The first party describes the problem from his point of view, expressing how the incident felt to him.
- Then the other party describes the problem from her point of view, expressing how the incident felt to her.
- The first person adds or clarifies information.
- The second person adds or clarifies information.

Step 3: Reach agreement

- The mediator asks what they would like to see happen. Each participant gives ideas.
- The mediator asks if the two disputants can live with these solutions.
- If they can, they sign a written copy of the agreement, shake hands, and return to class.

Step 4: Alternative to agreement

- If they cannot agree, the mediator guides the round robin for a few more minutes until they either come to consensus or are at a stalemate.
- If no compromise is reached, students are then dismissed from mediation with an imposed compromise, or they proceed through normal disciplinary channels.

Step 5: Express appreciation

- No matter the outcome, the mediator shakes the students' hands and earnestly thanks them for trying mediation.

Resolution skills have been shown to have a positive effect on academic achievement. Like class meetings, they teach students to articulate a viewpoint, listen to others' viewpoints, and brainstorm and evaluate potential solutions. These skills can be incorporated into the regular curriculum through guided practice (Bickmore 2011, 42).

As children move up through the grades, they can learn and apply developmentally appropriate conflict resolution skills. Primary level children can use a *peace table*, a special place in the classroom where students who are having a disagreement can come to a solution on their own. Intermediate level students have the maturity and judgment to serve as playground, cafeteria, and bus conflict managers for younger children. Late middle and high school level students can learn conflict resolution skills to prepare them to lead formal peer mediation. Local communities often have organizations dedicated to conflict resolution and skilled mediators willing to come into the school to train staff and students.

IN THE PRINCIPAL'S OFFICE

For one solid month, we all gave the concept of kindness some deep thought. We talked about it, practiced it, and recognized it in others. We wrote about it, sang about it, and looked for it in the stories we read. Our hope is that we internalized it and will act in kind and compassionate ways that make our school, homes, and communities good places to be. But don't worry. This is not the end of it. We will make sure being kind is always on our minds, every day, every year, until it becomes a part of who we are.

—Letter from the Principal

This letter, one of a series I sent home to families throughout the school year, was one way of conveying the message that I not only supported teaching children to be good people, I was a vigilant and visible leader of the movement.

Aristotle, who claimed "The best way to teach morality is to make it a habit with children," would applaud us for taking this duty seriously. The principal is a critical player and many believe the most important influence on the climate of the school. Every action or omission exposes and models the principal's belief system for students, families, and staff.

Discipline policies and procedures can be consistent yet treat each child as an individual and consider context, and be fair and proactive. When principals require students to take responsibility for their behavior and seek solutions and restitution they uplift "discipline" from punishment and imposed consequences to an opportunity to model and practice better behavior. *Teaching*, not punishing, is the business of schools. Good principals also use their authority to step in and intervene when something negative is going on in the school.

Principals have the positional and, hopefully, the personal power to make parents feel welcome in the school as important partners. There is no place for actions or policies that diminish the role of the parent, blame or belittle them, or make them feel less than respected. If parents are upset and agitated, the principal and teachers can use de-escalation strategies to calm them down. They employ empathy to see the situation from the parent's view and find ways to work together. These are the pro-social skills of a professional educator.

MAKING SCHOOL REAL

We can be creative and find ways to teach pro-social skills and community building within the current educational program and time constraints. It not only can be done, it turns out to be the most effective and natural way to get it done. Good literature and history have all the elements of life lessons embodied in the development of characters, the challenges they face, and the choices they make as they face them. Making our own connections to what we read and experience is essential to true learning.

Teachers do not need a mandate from a state education office to motivate them to structure teaching around the moral reasoning and choices of real and fictional people. Most teachers already know that the universal questions of life, along with individual concerns, hook students' interest and inspire them to learn more. What teachers may not realize is the need to be systematic, consistent, and tenacious in applying this critical thinking approach both inside and outside of the classroom.

The difference between *educating* and *schooling*, as John Dewey discussed, is students who are personally connected and committed to their community and to human beings as a whole. Therefore, it is important to offer children and young adults the chance to put new concepts into action. If we want our kids to be intrinsically motivated to do good works now and as adults, we need to provide them real life opportunities to practice.

Writing letters to the editor about a local issue, participating in community service projects, learning about and fulfilling a community need, cross-age tutoring, volunteering to work in the school cafeteria or library, and serving as kindergarten bus helpers and recess playground monitors all offer students valuable practice at being good people. This pro-social skill practice helps students to make healthy choices that benefit them and their community. They will already know what it feels like to be of service and to show compassion the next time a situation presents itself. It will become their way of relating to the world.

THE POWER OF A BELIEF-DRIVEN CULTURE

The notion that intrinsic motivation fueled by positive beliefs and values leads to strong character should be the foundation of everything we do with the children in our schools. While they are learning how to treat each other with respect and taking responsibility for their words and actions, they are creating the safe learning climate they need and deserve. All of this practice builds relationships that are critical for a sense of community and connectedness.

Our intentional efforts to improve the climate of the school will, in turn, change the culture of our school. The beliefs and attitudes become an integral part of who we are as teachers and parents, as children and schools, and as safe and caring communities. These central beliefs will never leave us as we teach children, make policy decisions, and work with each other. This requires a sustained commitment, one that touches the essence of who we are as a school community. There will be no program to blame or replace.

When students move through the educational system, they will know:

- Each of them is unique and has something to offer the world.
- Learning is exciting and hard work is rewarding.
- Adults do care about them and want them to do well.
- What they say and do is who they are.
- They have the power and responsibility to make good choices.
- If they make a mess, they have to clean it up.
- They must be true to what they believe is right.

Equations That Add Up
Positive climate + Engaging lessons = Connected, well-behaved students
Pro-social skills + Practice = Intrinsic motivation

Chapter 8

What is the Role of School Staff?

Everything a teacher does, as well as the manner in which he does it, incites the child to respond in some way or another and each response tends to set the child's attitude in some way or another.

—John Dewey

Positive relationships provide the basis for motivation and enjoyment. Students work hard for teachers who show them respect, make them laugh, and who can be trusted to care about them as individuals. Ask any adult and she will likely be able to point to one or more teachers who had a major impact on her life. People remember their special teachers for a lifetime. When asked to give three words or phrases that best describe the teacher who had the most positive influence in their life, the largest number of Americans responded with the word *caring*, followed by *encouraging, interesting, personable*, and of *high quality* (Bushaw and Lopez 2010, 15).

Society holds teachers to a high standard, and we are expected to be exemplary role models. The vast majority of teachers are just that. Students look up to us, and we can have a profound positive effect on their lives. Just as they remember their good teachers with fondness and appreciation, they remember with disdain those who were not respectful or kind and, even after much time has passed, with anger. We have all been through the educational system and know how true this is.

Teachers and parents are members of a special group called significant others. Significant others are people who, because of the loyalty and emotional attachment we enjoy in caring personal relationships, carry more weight than other adults the child barely knows. While teachers do not control what children experience, they have a tremendous influence as a role model and guide. Adults in a school with a healthy climate consistently and thoughtfully model what we expect from our students—mutual respect and non-violent solutions to problems—and use positive social skills all day as they work with students and each other.

DID I REALLY JUST SAY THAT?

It is true for our students and for us as well: what we say and do is who we are. As adults in the stressful situation of having authority over and responsibility for children, we are all likely guilty of using some form of negative behavior toward our students. And if we are not careful we can easily step over the line from positive discipline to the subtle forms of violence we listed on the continuum. This creates a kind of school bullying that comes from teachers and administrators. Having been in both positions, I understand how the responsibilities and power we have combined with the frustrations of teaching and running a school can make for a dangerous combination.

In the not so distant past corporal punishment was an accepted form of student management. Teachers used wooden canes, leather straps, and hickory switches to dominate children into compliance or to teach them a lesson. Even in the twentieth century misbehaving students were sent to the principal's office to be hit with a wooden paddle. It was not until 1973 that the first state, Massachusetts, finally outlawed corporal punishment. The most recent state to put an end to the use of this archaic form of discipline was Pennsylvania in 2005. Nineteen states still allow children to be punished physically.

A DUTY TO *DO* NO HARM

Teacher or principal violence toward students might not be a new concept, but connecting it to bullying prevention *is* a new development. With all the concern about bullying in schools, it is a natural progression to look at the behavior of the adults who work with students and who are entrusted with keeping them safe. It is a sensitive issue in great part because the teacher is the person with the tough job of maintaining order so she can teach. When students interfere with these responsibilities teachers might resort to bullying behaviors to end the disruption. It is difficult for many teachers to face losing some of the tools they use to run their classrooms.

But teachers and other school staff, because of our role as adults in a position of care and trust, have the responsibility to protect each child emotionally and physically. Consider the Supreme Court's 1999 ruling in

Davis v. Monroe County Board of Education affirming that schools receiving federal funds "may be held financially responsible where officials are 'deliberately indifferent' to harassing behaviors that are severe, pervasive, and objectively offensive." The lawsuit defined the criteria for school liability and it does not appear to matter who is doing the harassing.

1. School officials had actual knowledge of severe, pervasive, objectively offensive behavior.
2. School officials were deliberately indifferent to such conduct.
3. The school had control over the harasser and the context where the harassment occurred.
4. The school's response, or lack of response, was unreasonable given such knowledge. (McEvoy 2005, 4)

USING POSITIONAL AND PERSONAL POWER

Power bestowed to an individual by the position she holds is called *positional* power. People also have *personal* power, how they use their unique combination of temperament, beliefs, experiences, positive character traits, frailties and strengths.

Personal power comes from our belief that we have the tools to act respectfully and an expectation that we will be treated with respect. The more vulnerable and threatened children and adults feel personally, the stronger the chance we will invoke the flight or flight response and either steamroll others or be steamrolled. For example, consider how students often treat substitute teachers. Students recognize when we lack confidence or authority (you aren't our "real" teacher) and some see it as a green light to push our buttons. This happens when we are the least emotionally able to respond appropriately. Desperation and violence rise as power slips away from us. Part of preparing to be a teacher is looking inside ourselves to identify our buttons, face them, deal with them, and learn not to react impulsively.

Teacher-on-student bullying looks like what we have already described as student-on-student bullying, but with more emphasis on the power differential. As described by McEvoy (2005), it is "a pattern of conduct, rooted in a power differential, that threatens, harms, humiliates, induces fear, or causes students substantial emotional distress."

This bullying involves these four important aspects that are different from student-on-student bullying:

1. Students are a captive audience and cannot easily escape to protect themselves.
2. A teacher has positional power over students in his classroom and must maintain order, which can give the illusion that bullying behavior is necessary to do the job.
3. Students are expected to be respectful and subordinate to adults, so a student who fights back or stands up for himself may be subjected to further discipline.
4. If a teacher who is bullying is reported to the school, the teacher gets the benefit of the doubt. This is especially true if the student is one who acts out, is seen as different from his peers, or is labeled a troublemaker.

With the deck stacked in favor of the adult, most bullying by teachers will not be reported and the chances are good that nothing will be done if it is reported. In the "Teachers Who Bully Study: Patterns and Policy," one student who experienced bullying by a teacher explained his school's response: "People could complain until they were blue in the face, but nothing would be done unless the teacher was physically abusive, and they never were." This response is unfortunately quite common.

In the spirit of do no harm, it is only fair to consider a teacher or principal's dominating behavior to be *emotional violence,* rather than a legitimate method of disciplining students. We have a responsibility to apply the violence continuum concept to teacher behavior, especially in light of our goal of creating a positive climate for each child. When we do this we see that shaming, sarcasm, scapegoating, threatening, belittling, yelling, embarrassing, name calling, and ostracizing are some of the things teachers do—both intentionally and unintentionally—that are an abuse of their positional and personal power.

This is in addition to the 223,190 incidents of physical violence (including slapping, paddling, grabbing, and throwing) the U.S. Office of Civil Rights reports occurred in corporal punishment states in 2005–06. Of these incidents, African American students are victims of physical punishment at twice the rate for White students (Corporal Punishment in U.S. Schools 2005–06 2008).

In order to deal with teacher-on-student bullying, we must ask ourselves some difficult questions. What is the motive behind bullying behavior? What need are we trying to fulfill? What is the intent of the choices we make to fill that need? Do we want to embarrass a child in front of his peers, hurt him emotionally, or make him feel uncomfortable? Are we seeking to re-establish our authority, put him in his place, make him afraid of us, or have him serve as an example for others? Are we venting our frustrations so we can save face and get back to teaching?

Students and teachers want mutually respectful relationships. Feeling connected to an adult and the school is a critical protective asset for positive youth development. Middle and high school students do report they have a trusting respectful relationship with some teachers, but more students express concerns about a lack of respect where they are "put down" by adults in front of other students in the hall or classroom (Student Voices 2011).

Below is a list of some of the things teachers do that shame and hurt students.

Things we might say:

- Call a child a name—obnoxious, a brat, hopeless, stupid, annoying.
- Use sarcasm or teasing disguised as humor to put a child in her place.
- Tell a child to "shut up!"
- Draw attention to a child as an example of what *not* to do.
- Lose control and yell loudly at a child or speak through gritted teeth.
- Force a child to answer a rhetorical question such as "Do I have to hold your hand when we walk in the hall?"
- Use profanity.
- Tell off-color jokes.
- Make sexual comments or overtures to a student.
- Make a demeaning comment disguised as humor, such as, "Earth to Johnny. Is anyone home?"
- Threaten a child with an unrealistic and mutually unhealthy punishment such as "You will not have recess for a month!"

Things we might do:

- Discipline a student in front of the whole class in a demeaning way.
- Use height or strength to dominate a student physically.
- Get into a child's personal space.
- Yell and shake a finger at the child
- Let negative feelings for a child affect how we treat him.
- Pass out papers in order from highest grade to lowest or announce grades out loud.
- Post a detention list on the board with students' names in full view.
- Take something personal (not contraband) away from a student and not give it back.
- Send a child to sit in a lower grade classroom because he is acting like a baby, a first grader, etc.
- Rap a child on the head or slam a book on his desk as we walk by to startle him into paying attention.

- Ignore bullying behavior.
- Make a child tell the whole class why he has to sit by himself or miss recess.
- Throw something at a child to get his attention or to make him stop talking.
- Single out a child unfairly when we are frustrated.
- Assume a child was at fault without giving him a chance to explain.

How we might teach:

- Put students in competition with each other further alienating and stigmatizing those who are on the margin of their peer group.
- Not allow students to talk, ask questions, or move around.
- Lecture and present information with little student engagement.
- Give a student a poor grade as punishment.
- Compare one student's behavior or work with another.
- Embarrass a child who wasn't listening by making him answer questions he does not know how to answer.
- Let students pick their own team or learning group, reinforcing the pecking order of the popular kids and the outcasts.
- Tell a child that you give up on him or that he will never "get it."
- Get angry at the class's behavior and give them a pop quiz.
- Rip up a child's work and throw it a way.

THE ONES WHO DRIVE YOU CRAZY

Bullies boss; teachers correct and guide. Looking at the list of negative behaviors, there is a lot of bossing going on. While sharp directives might be expedient and let us continue teaching, they might also start a verbal power struggle between the student and us. They also treat students as adversaries to be conquered rather than children who need to be taught.

These tactics seduce us because they appear successful when the behavior stops right away.

Children and adults can be startled or demeaned into quick compliance. If we need to stop a child from hurting someone or getting hurt, of course we go ahead and yell his name sharply. But verbal darts used as a way to control students erode relationships and ruin the classroom climate for everyone. Bullying does emotional damage to the target (victim) and puts the rest of the students (bystanders) on edge, wondering when the next attack will occur.

Another form of psychological violence is the constant reprimanding of a particular student. We might hear these students' names repeated many times during a lesson or while the class is walking in the hall. Sometimes they will be sitting outside the classroom door looking sheepish as we walk by.

Their day may sound something like this:

- Johnny, I told you to sit down!
- Johnny, where is your social studies book? Did you forget it at home again?
- Johnny, everyone else is finished; why are you still on the second question?
- Johnny you never listen. Go sit in the back of the room until lunchtime!
- Johnny, I've had it with you! Go to the office!
- That's Johnny, all right; he's our class clown, always in trouble.
- Who got water all over the floor? Was it you, Johnny?
- Johnny, your name is already on the board. Do you want me to call your mother?

Imagine that Johnny is a student in your classroom. It is obvious that he is driving you crazy and he and the whole class know it. He knows he cannot make a move without being called out for it. He is beaten down when he needs to be lifted up. Students laugh at our sarcastic comments and tease Johnny about them after class. He is now the bad kid who is always in trouble, viewed with less respect as stupid or a problem child. He now has a reputation to maintain, a reputation that might be his only chance to feel like he has a place in the school.

Some children model what you have done and use Johnny as a scapegoat. They blame him when there is a disagreement and a problem is reported. Other students who have the positive qualities of empathy and compassion might feel sorry for him and lose respect for you as a teacher for treating him that way.

How does Johnny react to this badgering? Reactions vary and can change over time. He might get angry with his oppressor and vow to get even, act out more, or believe he is bad and that he deserves the mistreatment. If the bullying is because of a general dislike of Johnny and not for a specific prohibited behavior, he does not even know why he is being treated poorly. He gets into trouble for small things and cannot seem to do anything right in the teacher's eyes. He may withdraw emotionally and mentally from the negative classroom climate. He has been bullied and like all victims of bullying the effect is personally damaging. He might shut down, start doing poorly in his schoolwork, or skip class to get away from a place where he has no power and gets no respect.

Teachers can easily name the students who regularly draw negative attention or the specific classes that are more challenging than others. It is time to step back and assess how effective it is to call students out in front of the class to change the unwanted behavior, and how it affects our relationship with the student and the rest of the class. In the spirit of The New Golden Rule of Empathy and *model what you expect,* we should put ourselves in the child's shoes. We might have more compassion for the child if we considered how it would feel if the principal singled us out verbally at a faculty meeting because we were talking or walked in late, or if we were chastised because our students scored poorly on a standardized test.

A HOSTILE ENVIRONMENT

No matter how we spin it, bullying is not a legitimate student discipline or classroom management technique, just as it is not acceptable behavior for students. A teacher who bosses and derides her students is not modeling pro-social behaviors. This approach is not constructive and does nothing to make the child feel he belongs to the classroom community, one of the most powerful of our basic needs. We succeed only in inducing feelings of shame, guilt, fear, loneliness, embarrassment, anger, failure, weakness, and unworthiness, which separate the child even further from his peer group. How can a child learn in such a climate and how, in good conscience, can we do this to him?

Alan McEvoy (2005) clearly asserts how destructive bullying by teachers is: "[This threat] tends to be non-physical but nevertheless pervasive and powerful. As social beings, humans fear shunning and humiliation almost as much (if not more) as we fear physical harm. This means the threat of humiliation can be used as a weapon." To the student, this amounts to a "deliberate cruelty by persons in positions of authority."

The Title IX Act passed in 1972 addressed the issue of liability if a school or other organization allows sexual harassment that creates "a 'hostile

93%
15–23 year olds who believed that most students in their high school would agree on which teachers bullied students.
Study by McEvoy (2005)

environment' that denies students equal access to their education." The concept of a hostile environment is increasingly being applied to students being bullied in the school setting by students or adults. New Jersey and other states specifically include staff-to-student bullying in their school climate anti-bullying laws and policies. They recognize the power held by the significant adults in a child's life, and how their impact is magnified.

Teachers who participated in the "Teachers Who Bully Study" discussed the "mean, over-the-top behavior of colleagues and the continuation of unprofessional conduct." They were aware of the bullying happening in their schools. A code of professional ethics and policies would ensure that teachers and support staff are clear about the behaviors that establish a hostile environment for students. In addition, schools can create a system for reporting teacher bullying and tracking complaints. It is easier for all of us to live up to expectations when we know what they are.

Bullying is not the same as a disagreement between the teacher and student, or about a student who is causing a disruption. In the case of a disagreement, the student and teacher should discuss the problem and work out a solution together.

But with bullying there is nothing to work out and no disagreement to settle. Bullying by teachers is habitual repeated behavior directed toward students who are weaker or have less power, designed to dominate or break their spirit. We know not to tell a student being bullied by another student to "work it out" with his tormentor, so we cannot tell a student to work it out with the teacher. If a student reports teacher bullying she should be able to transfer to another class without penalty and be protected from retaliation.

A DUTY TO *ALLOW* NO HARM

The staff of a school is held accountable to both *do* no harm and to *allow* no harm to be done. In Student Voices (Jalloh 2004), students told us they want adults to intervene to stop bullying and harassment, and what adults can do to help them feel safe in school:

- Talk with students; institute programs that allow students to express themselves (ex. social workers, peer mediation).
- Create a more positive and relaxed environment with more enthusiastic teachers, and lessons and activities that are fun.
- Work with students to take responsibility for their own motivation, self-control, and studying.
- Increase attention to students' rights and respect for their property. They want teachers and administrators to do something about the illegal actions students do to other students.

• Create a climate where everyone learns to respect each other.

Students also say they specifically want us to protect them from what is a common cultural tradition in educational institutions: hazing. Hazing reverses the classic model of violence directed at someone who belongs to a group perceived to be of *lower status* or power. Hazing is violence inflicted on students because they want to belong to particular group they consider of *higher status*. Peer pressure and the desire to be accepted into an elite group motivate students to set aside their self-respect and quietly suffer humiliation and put themselves in danger.

Using a random sample of high school students throughout the country, a 2000 study by Alfred University asked students to complete a confidential questionnaire on their experiences with hazing. 48 percent of high school students admitted being hazed by school groups. The highest percentage of hazing was in sports teams, gangs, and other social groups, but, surprisingly, it existed in virtually all school groups. The study found both males and females were hazed, that male hazing more often involved dangerous behavior, and 40 percent of boys who were hazed would never report it (Hoover and Pollar 2000).

Where does hazing behavior reside on the violence continuum? Students being hazed in middle and high schools experience violence that includes humiliation, physical assault, battery, negligence, infliction of emotional duress, forced intoxication, and sexual assault and rape. This is neither dignified nor life affirming for the perpetrator, the victim, or for bystanders. At best it is an embarrassing situation with behavior that would never be tolerated under normal circumstances, and at its worst it is condoned violence and a crime.

What does hazing look like? The Alfred study defined three types of hazing behavior used by various school groups: humiliation, substance abuse, and dangerous hazing. This is a sampling of the kind of hazing violence reported in the United States from a single year. Students were:

• Spat on, hogtied, held in a locker and slammed into a wall.
• Dragged across a muddy field then made to stand against a wall while soccer teammates kicked balls at them.
• Roughed up, paddled, and then forced to box each other until they bled.
• Restrained with duct tape.
• Beaten by ten athletes until bruised.
• Sexually assaulted with foreign objects. (Jacobs 2000)

Students are also subjected to: tattooing, piercing, head-shaving, branding, sleep deprivation, physical punishment (paddling and "red-bellying"), and kidnapping (What is Hazing? 2011).

71%
Students subjected to hazing "reported negative consequences, such as getting into fights, being injured, fighting with parents, doing poorly in school, hurting other people, having difficulty eating, sleeping, or concentrating, or feeling angry, confused, embarrassed or guilty."
Hoover and Pollar (2000)

The Alfred study found less than a handful of school organizations *did not* haze new members—the school newspaper and yearbook for example—and that the rest—fraternities and sororities sports, gangs, music, art, theater, social, political groups, cheerleading, and church groups—had significantly high levels of hazing. Hazing is either kept under the radar of adult scrutiny, or adults are aware of it and do nothing (Hoover and Pollar 2000).

The Ohio State Education Department recognized the role schools play in the continuation of the tradition of hazing. Their code for hazing from the elementary through the college level is an inclusive definition and strong condemnation of hazing and the adults who allow it. The code warns that any adult who "recklessly" permits hazing, or who has knowledge of the hazing and takes no action to stop the behavior is liable for civil action for injury and damages, including mental and physical pain and suffering (Hazing Laws in Ohio? 2004). Adult culpability for what happens to their students is a wake up call to all middle and high school staff.

A majority of the students surveyed in the Alfred University study said they would not report hazing, but also look to the adults in charge to intervene on their behalf. When asked to identify the best prevention strategies, they revealed their dislike of hazing:

- 61 percent wanted strong disciplinary measures.
- 50 percent wanted police investigations and prosecution.
- 43 percent wanted to replace hazing with positive bonding experiences.
- 37 percent wanted adults and students to receive education about positive initiations and hazing.

- 30 percent wanted challenging activities instead of hazing.
- 29 percent preferred students to be asked to show good behavior to get into a group. (Hoover and Pollar 2000, 14)

The school has a direct supervisory role over the groups it sponsors and, therefore, the obligation to keep participants free from emotional trauma and physical harm. Schools can reduce hazing abuses by educating students, families, and school personnel, especially school coaches and extracurricular activity supervisors, and by enacting anti-hazing policies. Safe school climate efforts should send a strong anti-hazing message and ensure there is follow through if it is noticed or reported. Coaches should model non-violent character-building behavior to motivate their athletes, instead of perpetuating disrespect and aggression. Positive initiation, as opposed to hazing, that involves young people in fund-raisers, athletic games, and food events like picnics and banquets build a sense of community and were supported by most students in the survey.

WE ARE SIGNIFICANT

Surveyed students were perceptive when they said schools would never be able to stop hazing because it would take a breakdown of tradition and that changing a culture is difficult. But we have repeatedly proven we can change the climate and culture of a school. We know that one of the most effective ways is to take the stand that no violence, including teacher bullying of students or student bullying of each other, is ignored or tolerated.

Students want teachers to treat them with respect and to protect them. Earlier we noted we could improve the climate of a school if we replaced hurtful behaviors with alternative strategies for bringing about cooperation, compliance, and motivation. Students will notice these difference and their relationships with teachers will be strengthened. They will feel safer, protected from harm, enjoy adult relationships more, and be more motivated to participate and learn. By changing our own behavior, we could quickly turn around the climate of the classroom and the school to everyone's benefit.

Equations That Add Up
Power + Empathy = Respectful treatment of others

Chapter 9

How Can Diverse Communities Work Together to Improve School Climate?

If we were logical, the future would be bleak indeed. But we are more than logical. We are human beings, and we have faith and we have hope, and we can work.

—Jacques Cousteau

Here we are ready to begin an exciting new journey to create a safe school climate and raise smart *and* good people. We know why we need to do it and what it looks like, but where do we start? We need to move people from the inertia and comfort of their personal assumptions and beliefs, to group problem solving and planning that translates into positive action.

Institutions resist change. Yet people will support efforts if they have a personal connection to the mission and feel listened to. If teachers and families are going to take the effort to create a safe school climate seriously, they will need to be driven by a reason to care, and a shared vision.

This journey may seem daunting but we have a few powerful forces working for us. Parents and teachers already have concerns as they try to raise and teach children in today's complex society. Events over the past decade have shattered the concept of schools as safe havens. And now the law tells us we must do it. This legal expectation to do something to improve school climate may be the compelling motivator we have needed. However, it is important to remember that while it may serve to motivate people to get involved, it does not provide the intrinsic motivation required to do a good job and to stay with the effort over time.

It is not necessary for every member of the school community to be actively involved in the planning in order for the effort to be successful. As with all movements of change, people sort out into different levels of commitment:

we have the leaders (the building principal and teachers must be vocal and visible leaders), the doers who provide capacity, the sideline supporters who are waiting to see what the leaders and doers come up with, the late arrivals who eventually join the movement, the skeptics who are not sure this effort is necessary or will work, and the naysayers who think it is a waste of time and let you know it.

There is room for everyone, though we must be careful not to let the naysayers or skeptics stop us from doing what is right and necessary. Support for the mission will be broad and lasting if it is done in a thoughtful and inclusive way. A tide of support will build from the leaders and doers, spreading to the watchers and, hopefully, to the skeptics. Success is persuasive, especially when it is celebrated. Whether the naysayers ever join us is a matter of their personal and professional growth.

It is time to use what we value and believe to create principles and concepts that become the basis for our goals. This gives us structure as we carry out the process to develop an action plan. Once the plan has been thoughtfully implemented we can regularly evaluate the wisdom and effectiveness of our efforts, and challenge ourselves to do better. We will expand the realm of possibilities and dream of what we can do next. But this is only possible if we honor the process and let people create their own reason to care and join with us, whether actively or in spirit.

REACHING INSIDE TO FIND COMMON BELIEFS

People do not usually appreciate someone else making assumptions about them and handing down solutions they think are right for them, particularly if they were never consulted. Teachers also do not like to be handed "solutions" to questions that were asked and answered by someone else. Giving teachers a program to implement or sending us out on our own to *fix* the problem is not fair. Through both approaches we squander the opportunity to work together to identify concerns, reach an understanding, and evoke a lasting personal and professional commitment. We miss the chance to build respect for each other and go past the surface to explore what we truly believe.

The creation of a caring school culture that teaches children to be good people does not happen through random teachable moments, nor does it magically occur by following a pre-packaged program. Rather it grows from set of dreams and principles shared by a group of people and the trust that we have the answers inside us. As one parent involved in the Los Angeles First 5 LA Partnership for Families said about bringing parents into the school:

The way you approach someone about getting involved or offering help can either turn them on or off. [As a parent] when someone has an attitude that they're above me, it's tough to take. I appreciate situations where people can relate more as equals and it's consistent because that's the culture. (Growing and Sustaining Parent Engagement 2010, 2)

A safe place to begin the conversation is with a dream or concern discussed in a welcoming environment where everyone is treated with respect and appreciation. When we ask ourselves essential questions such as, "What do we want our children to be like? How would we describe a perfect life for them? What do we dream for them?" it helps us both to clarify our own thinking and to give us a group perspective. Asking these questions can bring about instant engagement because the questions are personal; everyone has a stake and an opinion and there are no right or wrong answers.

When you ask teachers and parents to conjure up the perfect life for their child or students, we are identifying a safe haven, what William Glasser calls our *quality world*. Think about what you would include in this quality world. Who would be there? Who and what would you keep out? This can be done as a group activity by drawing a large circle to represent our quality world. As components of a quality life are identified, the facilitator can write them inside the circle. The things that we would exclude are written outside of the circle.

We could also compare what people of diverse experiences consider a quality life and what they feel are harmful influences by making a T-chart to record people's ideas under the headings, *In Our Quality World, Out of Our Quality World*. The commonalities revealed by asking members what they value and are concerned with can unite the group. You now have a collection of universal hopes and expectations for children. as well as an understanding of the negative forces that create a toxic environment. The group has created a visual representation of the dream school climate and the ice is broken.

The list of elements excluded from our quality world will undoubtedly contain examples of violence. This can lead us into the foundation of all safe school efforts: the violence continuum activity.

ESSENTIAL QUESTIONS DRIVE OUR THINKING

One we complete the violence continuum activity described in chapter 3, we can use a brainstorming process to explore the essential questions, "What concerns us most about our children? and What does a good person look like? Essential questions are designed to engage us on a personal level so we cannot remain detached. They force us to take a hard look at the example we set and the lessons we teach. They ask us to have the insight to acknowledge what is right, as well as the courage to say what is lacking. Essential questions reconnect us with the power of our beliefs.

The nature and wording of the questions we ask is critical. Essential questions should open up honest dialogue and reveal our basic beliefs. Ask students, parents, staff, and teachers to define respect or another abstract concept, and they might struggle to put it into words. Ask them to describe what respect *looks like* in real life and the ideas will flow.

We have already asked the group to define a quality life. Now we can ask other essential questions such as:

- What is our school good at and how do we know?
- What are we *intentionally* doing to raise children who make thoughtful, informed choices?
- What meaningful experiences do we provide for students to practice being empathetic, honest and fair, altruistic, and all the other things we say we want them to be?

We can build the confidence people need to actively participate in the activity by using a *think-pair-share* approach. Members of the group first think about the essential question by themselves and jot down their ideas. The facilitator then invites them to discuss their ideas with a neighbor. After a few minutes they are asked to share their ideas with the whole group. This simple technique increases self-confidence and raises the likelihood that each person will speak out and be heard.

Exploration of an essential question and follow-up questions might go something like this:

- *What worries us about today's children?* (Too many kids think it is okay to use physical violence to settle an argument. The media seems to influence them more than we do.)
- *What do we want that we don't have?* (Time to talk to our children in the evening. Confidence that the school is a safe place.)
- *Why is this important to us?* (Today's teasing can easily turn into physical bullying. We want our children to believe in their own power to do good things. We want to continue to influence and protect our children as they grow up.)

The facilitator should write down the ideas as they are shared, type up the information to serve as a record of the ideas generated, and distribute them at the next gathering. This physical record of the group's hard work shows them that what they have to say is valuable and sets the stage for a continuing dialogue. It reinforces the underlying belief of the brainstorming process, the belief that we each have the answers inside of us.

THERE ARE NO SHORTCUTS

The importance of the steps outlined here cannot be overstated. Personal involvement gives us a stake in the outcome, a common purpose, and the motivation to continue. Brain research says that in order for new information to be remembered, it must make sense and have meaning for us. Asking essential questions leads teachers, parents, children, and community members to a dynamic and passionate dialogue. Our brains are satisfied that the work is worthy of our time and effort. And we are so very glad we were asked.

Unfortunately, these steps are the ones most often skipped as we rush to take action. It is a challenge to bring busy teachers and parents together and ask them to question their deeply held beliefs and assumptions. It is personal and requires individual effort in a world of an already overflowing educational agenda, looming high-stakes tests, and complicated family lives. We need to convince all parties that teaching children to be respectful and responsible is a high priority.

Something special occurs when people in a variety of roles and from a range of cultural and economic backgrounds share their feelings and beliefs in a respectful climate—they discover they share many significant core values and dreams. Once we take the time to find out who we are and what we want, we will know what to do. The specifics of how, when, and who are up to individual school communities that know the culture, population, school politics, and specific factors that will affect the success of their endeavor.

We base our efforts on these understandings:

➤ There are no pre-packaged solutions.

➤ The answers lie within our school community.

➤ Collaboration helps us define our direction.

➤ Over time, our systematic efforts reap systemic results.

OUR CIRCLE OF INFLUENCE

Essential questions may trigger a cathartic release of pent-up frustrations, along with a little venting and maybe some finger pointing. This is to be expected and even healthy. The mistake would be to let the conversation stay at this level. Instead, we need to foster a shift from a feeling of powerlessness to one of efficacy. We need to move the conversation from complaints and futility to the more positive approach of "what can we do to fix it?"

Some participants, such as the skeptics and naysayers and those who tried before and failed, may proclaim the problem is too big with too many negative forces working against us. They might argue that if only parents would teach their kids right from wrong, if only the media and video games would stop promoting disrespect and glorifying violence, or if the schools would just tighten up their discipline policies, there would be no problems. There is some merit to these challenges, but they are not excuses for doing nothing or for thwarting the honest efforts of those who want to try. The challengers likely do not understand the weight of their positional and personal power—their potent circle of influence.

When adults and children find their voice they discover their circle of influence is strong and expansive. We influence those around us who in turn influence those around them. As the message gets out, the work of a small group grows into something significant.

Equations That Add Up
Essential questions + Honest dialogue = Shared vision
Shared vision + Circle of influence = Efficacy

Chapter 10

How Do We Take Our Vision and Make It Happen?

Conviction is worthless unless it is converted into conduct.

— Thomas Carlyle

To take thoughtful action to improve school climate we need to gather information about the climate of *our* particular school, as experienced by *all* members of the school community. Once we identify the risks and protective assets we can make a plan. Each school is unique and requires and deserves an approach that fits and respects its culture. Which of these information-gathering strategies might work in your school? What if . . .

- We put a note in teachers' mailboxes announcing a breakfast meeting to talk about the climate of our school?
- The shared decision-making team put on their next meeting agenda the question of how school climate affects school violence and student achievement?
- We had the faculty create a violence continuum?
- We posed one of the essential questions at a parent-teacher or faculty meeting?
- We asked grade level teams to do the quality world activity?

Once essential questions are discussed, they will likely generate an urgency and motivation to *do something*. Now we are faced with what may be the most important, and quite possibly the most difficult, step in the process: to take that energy and harness it into purposeful and well-planned action. People may want to know if we really need to collect data to tell us what we have already agreed that we know: That our society is too accepting of violence, lacking in respect and ethical direction, and short on positive role models, and that schools can and must counter these influences and the everyday violence that happens as a result.

Our answer is that a plan must be more than emotion-driven, random action. Reaction without reflection leads to interventions that are simply layered on the status quo. After a flurry of initial interest and activity come small temporary gains, followed by disillusionment—at which point all positive momentum is lost. To do things right we need to gather information, raise awareness, build consensus, and develop a thoughtful, long-lasting, reasonable plan. However, it is important that this process move along at a pace that keeps the momentum going and the participants invested.

WHAT IS ON EVERYONE'S MIND?

How do we find out what members of our school community think? How do we know what we are doing well and where we need to improve? We ask them. There are many ways to solicit this information using surveys and questionnaires, including commercially prepared school climate surveys available on the Internet. We can also draft our own simple questionnaire to put in the school or district newsletter for parents to complete.

It is important to consider the approach we use to soliciting this information. Anonymous student surveys, especially when completed on the computer, are likely to elicit more honest answers and a better return rate than paper surveys handed out in class. A survey based on the violence continuum can uncover school community members' beliefs about what is okay and what is harmful, and can reveal what negative behaviors may have gone unchecked. One interesting approach is the "homework assignment" where all teachers in the school send students home with the task of conducting a short age-appropriate interview with their parents. What better way is there to connect school and home and remind parents that they do have a voice in their school.

Many resources are available that offer schools self-assessment tools and suggestions for how to plan and implement changes. These are not step-by-step programs but models and surveys offered free or for a nominal fee by federal and state education departments, national foundations, and interest groups.

Surveys offer a holistic view of the culture and climate of the school and can pinpoint what needs attention. The following sites are a good place to start searching for the survey right for your school.

- Available for no charge at the website of the Institute for Excellence & Ethics is a comprehensive battery of survey tools for students, staff, and

parents that look at assets (protective factors) provided by school and family culture. (http://excellenceandethics.com)
- Stopbullying.gov is an excellent site to browse 33 assessment scales available to measure bullying, victimization, perpetration, and by-stander experiences.
- The U.S. Department of Education's Office of Safe and Drug-Free Schools operates the online Safe and Supportive Schools Technical Assistance Center, which offers many resources including a School Climate Survey Compendium of student, staff, and family surveys that can be used as part of a school climate needs assessment. (*http://safesupportiveschools.ed.gov*)

SAMPLE SURVEYS

Comprehensive school safety/school climate assessments look at both the physical security and the social climate of the school, or at just one or the other, and are tailored for students, staff, and families. The sample surveys that follow are from a variety of sources and are representative of what is available online.

California School Climate and Safety Survey

This survey is designed to provide support to school site-based safety teams and is available at no cost. The survey asks students to indicate whether statements, such as the ones that follow, are true most of the time, sometimes true, or not usually true.

1. Our school is a comfortable place to learn.
2. Students treat each other with respect.
3. Students avoid using putdowns to hurt each other.
4. Students solve problems without fighting or using threats.
5. Students accept others who are different from them.(www.wested.org/cs/we/view/pj/245)

Ripple Effects School Safety Profiler

This survey is available at http://www.rippleeffects.com/needs and covers six areas based on the early warning signs of potential school violence as identified by the U.S. Departments of Education and Justice:

1. Discipline/school.
2. Respect for persons.

3. Presence of, or access to, weapons.
4. Presence of drugs or alcohol.
5. Students' ability to use social skills to handle challenging situations.
6. Student access to and confidence in community resources for problem solving.

Both student and teacher responses are solicited. For example, one item asks students to indicate how often (almost always, usually, sometimes, not often, or almost never) the following is true: "If I have a personal problem, I talk to a teacher or school counselor."

School as a Caring Community Profile-II (SCCP-II)

This survey from the Center for the 4th and 5th Rs by Tom Lickona and Matthew Davidson at the State University of New York at Cortland can be completed by school staff, students, and parents. Using a rating scale of 1 (*barely*) to 5 (*almost always*), the survey asks school members to rate thoughtful statements such as:

• Students care about and help each other, even if they are not friends.
• The school treats parents in a way that makes them feel respected, welcomed, and cared about.
• Students exclude those who are different (e.g., belong to a different race, religion, or culture). (http://www2.cortland.edu/dotAsset/289182.pdf)

Standards of the Heart

This aptly titled initiative from the Wisconsin Department of Public Education's *Characteristics of an Equitable School* intends to make all schools places where children feel safe and valued. The goal is to develop positive citizenship skills in the classroom, in extracurricular activities, and through the school climate under what they refer to as "planful" efforts. "Schools that foster standards of the heart have high expectations for students' behavior. They planfully provide a variety of curricular, co-curricular and extra-curricular opportunities that build strong personal and interpersonal skills." The Standards of the Heart can be changed from statements into questions and used to evaluate how members view the school:

• Provides a school that is safe, attractive and free from prejudice.
• The school environment fosters and promotes respect and caring.
• Discipline is firm, fair and consistent.
• School mascots, emblems, team names and logos are free from bias or stereotyping and do not perpetuate past discrimination.

- Pictures and information about diverse groups and cultures are exhibited.
- Orientation programs address the needs of all students and make every student feel welcome. (www.dpi.state.wi.us/cssch/csssoh1.html)

Once you have collected data using one or more tools, the next step is to analyze the data and find out what they tell us. Many organizations can analyze the raw data or your school may be able to enlist the help of a school psychologist, administrative intern, community member, or graduate level student at local university who has experience gathering and analyzing survey information. Depending on how complicated the survey and the level of data desired, some assessment tools could also be tallied and analyzed by the action plan group itself.

It is also important at this point to determine if we are in full compliance with what our school district, state, and the federal government require of us. School and district codes of conduct, discipline plans, school safety plans, professional development opportunities, and data on discipline should also be reviewed and factored into defining our needs and assets. They might even become the focus of our action plan.

LOOKING IN THE MIRROR

The data we have collected can be used to conduct a *force field analysis* — a simple self-assessment technique used to determine what is helping and hindering a school from meeting its safe school climate goals. The analysis begins by identifying a simple shared goal such as, "Our school is a safe and positive place for all children" or "Differences are respected by all and help make us a strong school community." A force field analysis is particularly effective at breathing life back into stale or forgotten—yet important—ideas or documents. If one is available, we can use our school mission statement or code of conduct as the focus of the force field analysis.

Goal: Our school is a safe and positive place for all children to learn.	
Forces PROMOTING Our Success	Forces PREVENTING Our Success

Keeping in mind the goal we have identified, we use the results of our data collection to answer two questions:

- *What is currently happening to promote our success?*
- *What are the barriers to our success?*

Begin with the forces promoting success and then move on to those preventing success. As in brainstorming, the facilitator listens to each idea and writes it down, asking for clarification or suggesting wording as appropriate. After the group is done identifying the forces, ask the members to look at each one of the barriers on the list and decide whether they have any influence over that item as either an individual or a group.

Mark the items the group feels it can influence with an asterisk so they can be used when deciding on action plan goals and objectives. This brings into play the concepts we have discussed including power, significant others, role models, circle of influence, commitment, and efficacy. As the group's dialogue evolves it may reveal that many of the barriers initially labeled as "out of our control," such as media violence or lack of parental involvement, really lend themselves quite well to action by individuals and school groups.

We are now ready—personally and as a group—to answer some core questions and make changes:

- *What messages do the practices and policies of our school send our students?*
- *Are these messages consistent with our beliefs?*
- *Are these messages consistent for all groups?*
- *If not, what can we do to improve?*

After this discussion, it is important to share the group's ideas with those who were not present. Face to face dialogue with all community members is ideal but unrealistic. Publicizing the work of the team can help to get people on the periphery thinking about creating a safe school climate and the role they might play in doing so. A school or district newsletter, website, or a special flyer can get the word out to a broad audience. Approached from the angle of, "When we asked our students how it feels to go to school here they said . . ." or "Parents would like their children to be able to . . .," an article conveys the message that the concerns and solutions being discussed come from our own parents, teachers, and students, and are specific to our school community. It also maintains the positive, non-accusatory tone that is necessary to garner support, and might just inspire some new members to join the team.

Other ways to get out the information are:

- Arrange for all school personnel to participate in the violence continuum activity.
- Publish the results of the brainstorming sessions.
- Submit quotes or brief articles to the school newsletter.
- Advertise it on the school website.
- Sponsor a motivating assembly for students and parents.
- Make a presentation to the school board.
- Make it obvious with posters and bulletin boards throughout the school.
- Send students home with catchy signs to put on the refrigerator.
- Talk about it at parents' curriculum nights and open houses.
- Arrange for publicity from the local media.

Implicit in these efforts is a confidence that reducing violence through a positive school climate is something everyone cares about.

CREATING AN ACTION PLAN

Now it is time to take action using a strategic planning model that identifies goals, objectives, and concrete initiatives. This puts the messy work of change into a manageable framework and ensures your ideas to improve school climate will not get lost. With a balance between idealism and pragmatism, the resulting action plan is simple, homegrown, and doable. It allows grassroots capacity and leadership to develop as members of the school community volunteer to spread the word, organize an effort, serve on a committee, and build lasting-relationships with each other.

The plan is tailored to the needs and strengths of our particular school and follows these tenets:

- Our planning efforts are driven by an overarching motivation to improve school climate.
- Goals are broad statements of long-term success, rather than specific tasks we can achieve.
- The risks and protective assets, concerns and attitudes we uncovered in our data collection process determine our broad goals and specific objectives.
- Action-oriented objectives target ways we can measure whether we have attained our goals.
- Clearly defined initiatives and activities, a timetable for implementation, the persons responsible, and an assessment component provide the means to reach these objectives.

- With enthusiasm and optimism, we put the plan into action in our school and homes.
- We revisit, review, and revise our efforts honestly and regularly.

The action plan development stage is exciting because it satisfies the drive to use what we have learned to make an impact. It represents the group vision by illustrating how we will get from where we are to where we want to be. The exact layout of the plan is not critical, though a simple chart is easy to work with. What matters most is that we have a commitment in writing to take action and a plan that identifies:

1. What we specifically want to accomplish.
2. How we are going to accomplish it.
3. When we will accomplish it.
4. Who is responsible for making it happen.
5. How we will know if we are successful.
6. What we will do to maximize our success.

The action plan should consist of goals, objectives, and activities. When developing your action plan, start with a goal that has a strong likelihood of success. Identify one easily attainable, yet meaningful, goal drawn from the ideas revealed in the violence continuum activity, surveys, meetings, dialogues, and the force field analysis. For example, our survey might have revealed that parents do not feel comfortable coming to school to talk with teachers about their children. Research and experience tell us that schools where parents are welcome, active partners are safer and more effective places to learn. Therefore, we may choose to implement changes to make the school more approachable to parents.

Broad Goal: Parents and teachers work together as a team.

Specific Objectives:

- The building is welcoming to parents.
- All parents participate in parent-teacher conferences.
- Parents attend special events and volunteer in the school.
- Parents reinforce the school's efforts to teach pro-social skills.
- Parents contribute ideas to help their children succeed in school.

Activities to reach these objectives:

- The "All visitors must report to the office." entrance sign is changed to a more colorful and friendly invitation: "Welcome to our school. Please make the office your first stop."
- Office staff makes a concerted effort to give parents a smile and warm greeting when they enter the office.
- Teachers and parents work together to identify the things they can do to have a successful discussion about the child.
- Parent-teacher conferences are made more attractive by sending parents personal invitations created by their children, offering evening hours, and scheduling individual conferences for parents who are raising a child separately.
- During parent-teacher conferences, we offer free on-site childcare, comfortable adult-sized chairs in which parents can wait, and a table set out with coffee and cookies.

Compare this plan to what one of my young, enthusiastic graduate students in my character education course described as her school's character education initiative. She explained that her school was a pilot school for character education in her district and that they were in the middle of their first year. She showed us a spiral bound manual that was two inches thick and flipped through the pages of all the activities it contained. When I asked what the district had done to prepare the teachers for such an important undertaking she replied, "Nothing." The building principal had simply handed out the manual on the first day of school and told the teachers to use it.

This attempt at character education is doomed to fail. It lacks the sense of unity and purpose that we know is crucial. It most likely does not use a common definition of violence. Minus context, motivation, and relevance, it is the dreaded *new program,* one more layer on the curriculum heap. It has little or no personal meaning for the teachers and, as a result, little chance of longevity. It is a money and time waster that likely won't make it to year two. In the meantime, it gives teachers and administrators the false impression that what they are doing is teaching students to be better people and making the school a safer place. But we know this is not how we make lasting changes to the climate and culture of our schools.

NOT AS COMPLICATED AS WE THOUGHT

The changes specified in our action plans are not big projects, programs, or activities. They are simply examples of acting on our beliefs by using and expecting kinder and more inviting ways of relating to each other. Some are gestures of consideration and goodwill that improve the climate and provide alternatives to hurtful behaviors.

The efforts needed to meet our goal of improving parents' feelings about coming to the school do not require much, if any, money, do not encroach on instructional time, do not take months to organize, and do not require permission from the school board. They are fundamental, low-key changes that make school a more inviting place for the families of our students, which, in turn, improve school relationships. In this way, changing the school climate will naturally lead to a change in school culture.

Consider another goal that might be part of the action plan, one that serves to remind the adults in the school community of their position as role models: "Teachers and administrators consistently model the behavior they expect from students." The action plan seeks a commitment by teachers, administrators, and staff to consciously model the life skills, character traits, and pro-social communications they expect from children. To do this, our action plan might arrange a discussion at a faculty/staff meeting or a PTA meeting, along with a newsletter article focusing on these essential questions:

- Are role models chosen?
- For whom are you a role model?
- What qualities would you like to see in your children?
- How can you model those qualities?

Another goal could be "Teachers take care of all students in the school." Awareness activities for staff can drive home the message to each of us that every child in the school is "my child," and that we need to look out for all students' welfare and personal growth. An action plan designed to remind staff members that every student is their responsibility leads them to intentionally and consistently treat them with dignity, to intervene to keep them emotionally and physically safe, and to model desired skills, attitudes, and behaviors.

The beauty of the action plan approach is that what we do with conscious intent at first, such as a pledge to smile and say hello to students we pass in the hall, eventually becomes an unconscious habit, ingrained in our behavior. Since we do act unconsciously a good deal of the time, we might as well have unconscious habits that benefit our children. This changes our view of students and reminds us that they are children. Students begin to feel that they belong to a caring school community of adults who want them to feel safe and will be there for them whenever they need help.

TAKING THE PLAN INTO OUR HOMES AND CLASSROOMS

A group of practicing teachers and I once looked at the Search Institute's "40 Developmental Assets for Elementary Children" and identified the five assets most important to our own success in life, which are missing in the lives of children today. The asset that came in at the top of our list was Asset #1, *"Family life provides high levels of love and support."* Parental support is a widely valued pillar of education and varies greatly. Acknowledging the importance of families does not absolve us from sharing responsibility for the way children turn out. Rather, it further underscores the power of schools to engage families to benefit their children.

The most important message we can send parents is that we truly care about their children. Parents benefit from learning good parenting skills and from being involved in their children's education. How readily they are willing to work with us and accept our help depends on the relationship we build between us. Parents need our help—and we need theirs—to do the best job possible teaching their children.

How do we move from *respect* to a deeper relationship of *trust* with parents and guardians? First we have to care enough about the relationship to try. Following the path from respect to empathy to compassion to trust is how we ensure successful parent-teacher interactions, both formal and informal. We see how important it is to put ourselves in other person's place and use that information to everyone's advantage.

Building Trust

The progression goes like this:

Respect *– I value you as a person.*

   Empathy *– I feel what you feel; I see the situation from your prospective.*

      Compassion *– I think and act in ways that show I understand and care.*

         Trust ... earned with respect, empathy, and compassion over time.

We want school to be one of our parents' favorite places, not a place to fear or avoid. It helps to invite families into school to see the school climate plan in action and send home newsletters, notices, and materials children have made. The school code of conduct we send them might wind up as the code of conduct for the family as well.

OUR ULTIMATE GOAL

Our ultimate goal is to weave the mission to teach children to be good and smart tightly into classroom instruction and school life. The individual classroom is where the plan ultimately succeeds or fails and the teacher, with support from the principal, holds the key. The answer to the content and time dilemma lies in embedding the intent to raise good people as deeply as the intent to teach children to read. The best action plan is one that fits seamlessly into the functioning of school and classroom life. It is not only *what* we teach, it is blended into the *way* we teach.

As with all dynamic organizations, we will only succeed if we continually measure our efforts against our belief system and goals, and refine, revise, and revive our plan as needed. Most importantly, we must remember to celebrate our successes. In this new safe school climate, we know we have been successful when we can say, "*We don't do that here; we treat people with respect.*" and our students, staff, and parents understand exactly what we mean.

Equations That Add Up
Information + Thoughtful analysis = Effective action

Chapter 11

How Do We Ensure the Changes Are Real and Lasting?

Any man's life will be filled with constant and unexpected encouragement if he makes up his mind to do his level best each day.

—Booker T. Washington

We have come full circle. We have looked at the purpose of schools, learned about violence in all its forms, identified the responsibilities we have to our students, and explored ways to bring people together to define our strengths and needs. And now we have ideas for how to get started. If this book has been successful, we feel more confident to do what before might have seemed impossible: create a safe and caring school climate where all children can learn in peace.

With this vision of what is possible comes the courage to acknowledge when something is wrong in our school, our classroom, our home, with us, or with our child, and that we need to make a change. We know better than to accept the dismissal of those who tell us not to worry about the subtle forms of violence, that it is just kid stuff, a part of our culture. We know not to believe the most discouraging and inaccurate words we can hear: we can't do anything about it anyway. The courageous among us look toward the promise of the future and the realities of today and choose to take action. Then we stick with it as long as it takes to bring the ideal to life and embed it in our culture.

UNITED BY BELIEFS

Throughout this book we are reminded to never underestimate the power of speaking from the heart and acting with conviction to change the world. When we ask essential questions we will be amazed at the insight adults and children have tucked away inside, waiting to be expressed. Committing to a set of beliefs, and articulating and modeling those beliefs as an individual or a group, influences others and affects the society in which we live. The foundational belief is that we have the obligation, insight, and influence to make school a better place for our children. Anything less is not an option.

We have learned a great deal about making sure our efforts to improve school climate are real and lasting. We can be creative and find ways to teach pro-social skills and community building within the current educational program and time constraints. It not only can be done, it turns out to be the most effective and natural way to get it done.

Our efforts are guided by our belief in our responsibility and ability to do something constructive:

- Schools have a mandate to teach students to be smart *and* good people.
- Our sense of efficacy and our circle of influence give us the power to effect positive changes.

Our belief in the power of relationships:

- Mutual respect and tolerance toward others is the foundation of non-violence.
- Empathy allows us to view life from the other person's point of view.
- School climate and student learning are a product of the relationships between students and teachers.
- Principals set the tone for the school and teachers set the climate of their classrooms.

Our belief that violence does exist in our schools:

- Violence is a continuum of behaviors and they are all destructive.
- We need to consistently address violence in all its manifestations.
- The hidden curriculum, the intentional and unintentional hurtful things we do, and the messages we send, can undermine a safe school climate.

Our belief that all children can learn:

- Children can learn to replace negative behaviors with pro-social behaviors.
- Successful safe school climate efforts focus on prevention by teaching pro-social skills.
- We can avoid future problems if we identify potentially dangerous students and those likely to be victims, and then intervene early and constructively.

Our belief that families and schools can work together:

- We build trust by welcoming and listening to others people's dreams and concerns with an open and caring mind.
- We reduce school violence through posing essential questions that allow people the time to examine their personal belief system, and then define the changes we need to make.
- A partnership with parents benefits children and affects how successful we are teaching them.

Our belief that the best solutions come from inside of us:

- We know the unique nature of the climate and the culture of our school and what we want for our children.
- Real change must be intrinsic; superficial interventions result in superficial changes that do not last.
- A simple action, such as modeling what we expect, often produces profound results.
- We never stop dreaming of what could be and trying to do better.
- We need to describe and feel our beliefs and make a promise to be true to them.

DESCRIBE IT

Our safe school climate efforts recognize that empathy and respect for others are the foundation of peace. The quality world we discuss gives us a vision of what could be. Even my elementary school children had a picture of a respectful, caring world, and told us that respect means:

- Helping people, talking nicely, playing nicely, and showing you care (Kindergarteners).
- Being nice to each other and sharing, helping, caring, being kind, and loving each other (1st graders).
- Knowing we all make mistakes and no one is perfect and using teamwork (3rd graders).
- Treating others the way we want to be treated, working things out between people, and showing consideration for people and their belongings (4th graders).
- Sharing, listening, being kind, helping each other, keeping the school clean, and behaving nicely (Resource Room students).
- Caring for and helping others including teachers, fellow students, family members, and any other people you spend time with, and respecting yourself by taking care of your body and sticking to your beliefs (5th graders).

FEEL IT

Metaphors help us clarify what we feel and believe so we can better understand and adhere to our mission. They bring concepts to a deep internal level where they become a part of us. When I was a principal, this is what the teachers in my elementary school said about respect:

- Respect is like a river . . . it is ongoing and flows from person to person
- Respect is like a sailboat . . . all the elements have to work in harmony
- Respect is like a rose . . . under the right conditions, it blooms
- Respect is like a butterfly . . . it is delicate
- Respect is like a balloon . . . it cannot reach its full potential unless you put effort into it
- Respect is like a candle . . . it is a guiding force

MAKE A PROMISE

As we have discovered, beliefs are what give us a vision and drive real change. Without beliefs to guide us, we will try anything, and without consensus on those beliefs we have trouble moving our vision forward. My teachers then took their respect metaphors a step further to create belief statements.

We Believe . . .

- Respect is everyone's right and responsibility.
- Self-respect and respect for others need to be modeled and are essential for growth.
- Respect requires mutual effort from all parties (students, teachers, parents, administrators, and the community), and is essential to a positive working environment.
- Mutual respect requires an understanding of differences.
- Respect is the linchpin of the whole educational system and the medium through which each member contributes and functions.
- Respect needs to be valued and nurtured.

They then made this promise:
    Let's keep the river flowing,
        the sailboat afloat,
            the rose watered,
                the butterfly flying,

the balloon full,
and the candle lit.

Our children are waiting for us to make their world physically and emotionally safe. They know it is up to us. When we accept that responsibility and summon the courage to do something about violence—something belief driven and long lasting—we make the climate and culture of our school community all they should be. When we do this everyone will celebrate. They will celebrate because we are keeping the promise that school is a safe haven for our children.

Equations That Add Up
Essential questions + Honest dialogue = Shared vision
Shared vision + Circle of influence = Lasting change

Glossary of Violence Terms

- Assault: an unlawful physical attack upon another; an attempt or offer to do violence to another, with or without battery, such as holding a bat in a threatening manner.
- Bashing: unprovoked physical assaults against members of a specified group such as gays and racial and ethnic minorities.
- Battery: unlawful beating or wounding of a person or touching in a hostile or offensive manner.
- Bias: prejudice; a particular tendency or inclination.
- Body slam: wrestling move in which an opponent is lifted and hurled to the ground, landing on his or her back.
- Dirty look: a facial expression of anger, disapproval, or disgust.
- Denigrate: to belittle someone, to treat them as if they lack value or importance.
- Discriminate: to make a distinction in favor of or against a person or thing on the basis of group, class, or category rather than according to actual merit.
- Disparage: to speak of or treat in a negative way; to belittle.
- Embarrass: to cause confusion and shame and make uncomfortably self-conscious.
- Exclude: to keep out.
- Extort: to take money, information, or another resource from a person by violence, intimidation, or abuse of authority such as force, torture, or threat.
- Glare: to stare at fiercely or angrily with a piercing look.
- Gossip: a conversation involving malicious talk or rumors about other people.

- Hate crime: a crime, usually violent, motivated by prejudice or intolerance toward a member of a gender, ethnic, racial, religious, or social group.
- Hate incident: an individual occurrence or event motivated by prejudice or intolerance.
- Haze: to abuse through humiliation, ridicule, and physical acts.
- Intimidate: to make timid and fill with fear.
- Libel: anything written that is defamatory or that maliciously or damagingly misrepresents a person.
- Menace: to threaten directly.
- Misogyny: hatred, dislike, or mistrust of women.
- Name-calling: verbal abuse, especially as a crude form of argument.
- Put-down: a remark or act intended to humiliate or embarrass someone.
- Retaliation: returning like for like, especially evil for evil.
- Ridicule: to make fun of.
- Rob: to take something from someone by unlawful force or threat of violence.
- Rumor: a story or statement in general circulation without confirmation or certainty as to facts.
- Sarcasm: a sharply ironical taunt or cutting remark.
- Scapegoat: a person or group made to bear the blame for others or to suffer in their place.
- Sexual assault: illegal sexual contact that involves force upon a person without consent or is inflicted upon a person who is incapable of giving consent.
- Sexual harassment: unwelcome directing of sexual remarks, looks, and unnecessary physical contact at a person.
- Slander: a malicious, false, and defamatory statement or report.
- Stalk: to pursue persistently without invitation or approval, and sometimes attack.
- Stare: to cause someone to become uncomfortable by looking steadily at them.
- Stigmatize: to put some mark of disgrace upon.
- Tease: to irritate or provoke with persistent petty distractions or other annoyance, often as "fun."
- Taunt: to mock in a sarcastic, insulting, or jeering manner.
- Vandalism: deliberately mischievous or malicious destruction or damage of property.

References

"10 Warning Signs." 1999–2009. Ripple Effects. Accessed March 10, 2011. www .rippleeffects .com/needs/warning_signs.php.

"2007 Annual National Crime Victimization Survey." US Education Department National Center for Educational Statistics (NCES). Accessed April 5, 2011. bjs. ojp.usdoj.gov/ content/pub/pdf/cv07.pdf.

Ali, Russlynn. 2010. "Dear Colleague Letter." U.S. Department of Education Office of Civil Rights. October 26. Accessed March 11, 2011. www2.ed.gov/about/ offices/list/ocr/letters/colleague-201010.htmlp.53.

"Anti-Bullying/Anti-Harassment: Legal Requirements." 2011. Iowa Department of Education. Accessed June 21, 2011. educateiowa.gov.

Assembly No 3466. 2010. State of New Jersey. November 15. Accessed June 21, 2011. www.njleg.state.nj.us/2010/Bills/A3500/3466_S1.HTM.

Barlow, Zeke. 2011. "Friend of King Spars With Defense Attorney in McInerney Murder Trial." *The Ventura County Star* July 8. Accessed July 8, 2011. www .vcstar.com/news/2011/jul/08/no-headline—-mcinerney_day_4/#ixzz1RYh2kYuj.

"Better Together." 2008 Annual Report America's Promise Alliance. Accessed June 28, 2011. www.americaspromise.org/About-the-Alliance/Press-Room.

Bickmore, Kathy. 2011. "Keeping, Making, and Building Peace in School." *Social Education*. Jan/Feb 2011 vol. 75–1, pp. 40–44.

Boccanfuso, Christopher and Megan Kuhfeld. 2011. "Multiple Response, Promising Results: Evidence-Based Nonpunitive Alternatives to Zero Tolerance." *Research to Results: Child Trends* March. Accessed March 1, 2011. www.childtrends.org/ Files/Child_Trends-2011_ 03_01_RB_AltToZeroTolerance.pdf.

Bradshaw, Catherine P. and Tracy Evan Waasdorp, Lindsey M. O'Brennan, Michaela Gulemetova. 2010. "Findings From the National Education Association Nationwide Study of Bullying: Teachers' and Education Support Professionals' Perspectives." National Education Association. Accessed March 6, 2011. www

.nea.org/assets/img/content/Findings_from_NEAs_Nationwide_Study_of_ Bullying.pdf.

Bushaw, William J. and Shane J. Lopez. 2010. 42nd Annual Phi Delta Kappa/Gallup Poll of the Public's Attitudes Toward Public Schools. Accessed June 2011. www .pdkintl.org/kappan/poll.htm.

"California Healthy Kids Survey." 1999. California Education Department. Accessed June 3, 2011. www.wested.org/cs/we/view/pj/245, p.77.

California School Climate and Safety Survey. n.d. Accessed April 10, 2011. web. me.com/michaelfurlong/MJF-Home/School_Climate_Safety_Survey.html.

Carroll, Joseph. 2007. "The Divide Between Public School Parents and Private School Parents." Gallup News Service. September 5. Accessed June 22, 2011. www.gallup.com/poll/28603/divide-between-public-school-parents-private-school-parents.aspx.

"Case Study: South Carolina Department of Education." n.d. Non-Violent Crisis Intervention. Accessed June 30, 2011. www.crisisprevention.com/CPI/media/ Media/Resources/casestudies/ South_Carolina.pdf.

"CDC Understanding School Violence Fact Sheet." 2008. Center for Disease Control and Prevention. Accessed May 2011. www.cdc.gov/ncipc/dvp/YVP/SV_Fact-sheet.pdf.

"Character Above All." n.d. Public Broadcasting System. Accessed June 30, 2011. www.pbs.org/newshour/character/quotes/.

"Children's Exposure to Violence." 2010. *Child Trends*. Accessed June 2011. www .childtrendsdatabank.org/alphalist?q=node/356.

"The Condition of Education: Overview." 2011. Report from National Center for Educational Statistics. Accessed March 2, 2011. nces.ed.gov/programs/coe/.

"Corporal Punishment in U.S. Schools 2005–06." 2008. The Center for Effective Discipline. Accessed July 9, 2011. www.stophitting.com/index. php?page=statesbannin.

Curwin, Richard L. and Allen N. Mendler. 1998. *Discipline with Dignity*. Alexandria Virginia: Association for Supervision and Curriculum Development.

"Cyberbullying: What Kids, Teens, and Adults Can Do." n.d. US Department of Health and Human Services, Department of Education, and Department of Justice. Accessed June 22, 2011. www.stopbullying.gov/topics/cyberbullying/ young_people/index.htm.

"Cyberbullying or Cyberthreat Situation Review Process." 2005. Center for Safe and Responsible Internet Use. Accessed July 9, 2011. www.d91.k12.id.us/Parentinfo/ CyberbullyingResouces.pd.

"Cybersafety 10 Tips." n.d. NYSCSS. Cyber Safety. n.d. New York State Center for School Safety NYSCSS. Accessed June 16, 2011. nyscenterforschoolsafety.org/ files/filesystem/factsheet4_cyberbullying.pdf.

Davis, Michelle R. 2011. "Schools Tackle Legal Twists and Turns of Cyberbullying." *Education Week: Digital Directions*. February 4. Accessed July 9, 2011. www .edweek.org/dd/articles/2011/02/09/ 02cyberbullying.h04.htm.

Dewey, John (1916). *Democracy in Education: An Introduction to the Philosophy of Education*. Chapter 2 pp.12–26. New York: Macmillian. Google Books edition. books.google.com.

"Early Warning-Timely Response: A Guide to Safe Schools." 2001. U.S. Department of Education and U.S. Department of Justice: Center for Effective Collaboration and Practice. Accessed April 28, 2011. cecp.air.org/guide/files/3.asp.

"Efficacy of Schoolwide Programs to Promote Social and Character Development and Reduce Problem Behavior in Elementary School Children." 2010. National Center for Education Research. 2010. Presented at the Social and Character Development Research Consortium. October 2010. U.S. Department of Education. Accessed March 16, 2011. ies.ed.gov/ncer/pubs/ 20112001/ pdf/20112001.pd.

"Five Promises." 2009. America's Promise Alliance. Accessed June 21, 2011. www. americaspromise.org/About-the-Alliance/Five-Promises.aspx.

Fox, James A. and Jack Levin. 2010. "Overreacting to School Shootings Intensifies the Problem." W1D World One Directory Free Online Research Papers. Accessed March 10, 2011. www.w1d.net/ /school-violence/overreacting-to-school-shootings-intensifies-the-problem/.

Gallup Student Poll. 2011. National Conference of State Legislatures. Accessed June 21, 2011. www.ncsl.org/default.aspx?tabid=19810.

Garbarino, James. 1999. *Lost Boys: How Our Sons Turn Violent and How We Can Save Them*. New York: The Free Press.

Garbarino, James. 2010. "Bullying: Poisonous Pedagogy." Transcript of keynote address presented at the Children, Youth and Families at Risk Conference (CYFAR). May 2010. Accessed May 23, 2011. www1.cyfernet.org/cyfar2010/keynote.html.

"GLSEN 2005 National School Climate Survey Sheds New Light on Experiences of Lesbian, Gay, Bisexual and Transgender (LGBT) Students." 2009. Accessed June 17, 2011. www.glsen.org/cgi-bin/iowa/all/news/record/1927.htm.

"GLSEN 2009 National School Climate Survey: Nearly 9 out of 10 LGBT Students Experience Harassment in School." 2009. Accessed June 1, 2011. www.glsen.org/ cgibin/iowa/all/library/ record/2624.html?state=research&type=research.

Grasmick, Nancy S. 2006. "Maryland: Confronting Classroom Bullies" *Leadership Insider*. National School Boards Association. August 2006. Accessed June 15, 2011. www.nsba.org/ site/docs/39100/39055.pd.

"Growing and Sustaining Parent Engagement." 2010. First 5 LA. The Center for the Study of Social Policy. Accessed July 3, 2011. www.cssp.org/publications/ growingandsustainingparentengagementtoolkit.pd.

Hamburger, Merle E. and Kathleen C. Basile, Alana M. Vivolo ed. 2011. "Measuring Bullying, Victimization, Perpetration, and By-Stander Experiences: A Compendium of Assessment Tools." Center for Disease Control and Prevention. www. stopbullying.gov/community/ tip_sheets/assessment_tools.pdf.

"Hazing Laws in Ohio?" 2004. Ohio High School Athletic Association. Accessed June 4, 2011. www.ohsaa.org/RTG/Resources/hazing/Law.htm.

Hoover, Nadine and Norman Pollar. 2000. "High School Hazing: Executive Summary Who is at Risk for Being Hazed?" Alfred University. Accessed March 23, 2011. www.alfred.edu/hs_hazing/.

Horton, Erica and Richard Locker. 2011. "Law Tough on Cyber Bullies in Tennessee." *Chattanooga Times Free Press,* June 11. Accessed June 21, 2011. timesfreepress. com/news/2011/jun/11/law-tough-cyber-bullies/.

Houk, Kimberly. 2011. "Hazing at Logan Middle School" Salt Lake City Utah, ABC4 news. May 25, 2011. Accessed June 15, 2011. www.abc4.com/content/news/state/ story/Hazing-at-a-Logan-middle-school/K7uk2xIe2EeyQZKwRNkehQ.cspx.

"How Many Youth Experience Each Asset?" 2002. The Search Institute. Accessed June 24, 2011. www.search-institute.org/research/assets/assetfre.

Hutton, Thomas. 2006. "No Rite of Passage: Coming to Grips with Harassment and Bullying." National School Boards Association *Leadership Insider*. August 2006. Accessed March 23, 2011. www.nsba.org/site/docs/39100/39055.pdf.

"Indicators of School Crime and Safety 2004: Discipline Problems Reported by Public Schools." National Center for Educational Statistics. Accessed June 21, 2011. nces.ed.gov/pubs2005/crime_safe04/indicator_16.asp.

"Indicators of School Crime and Safety." 2005. National Center for Education Statistics. Accessed June 21, 2011. nces.ed.gov/programs/crimeindicators/ crimeindicators2005/.

"Indicators of School Crime and Safety 2009." National Center for Educational Statistics (NCES). Accessed March 10, 2011. nces.ed.gov/programs/ crimeindicators/crimeindicators2009/key.asp.

Jacobs, Andrew. 2000. "Violent Cast of High School Hazing Mirrors Society, Experts Say." *New York Times* March 5. Accessed June 22, 2011. www.nytimes. com/2000/03/05/nyregion/violent-cast-of-school-hazing-mirrors-society-experts-say.html.

Jalloh, Mary G. 2004. "Student Voices: A Five-Year Study of Student Ideas on Improving Learning, School Safety, Risk-Prevention, and Relationships." New York State Center for School Safety: Research Brief. Accessed June 7, 2011. nyscenterforschoolsafety.org/files/filesystem/brief4.pdf.

Jalloh, Mary G. 2009. "Literacy as a Violence Prevention Strategy." New York State Center for School Safety: Issues Brief. December. Accessed May 15, 2011. nyscenterforschoolsafety.org/ files/filesystem/literacy.pd.

"Jock Privilege." n.d. *Teaching Tolerance*. Accessed April 29, 2011. www.tolerance. org/supplement/ jock-privileg.

Kohn, Alfie. 2011. "How Education Reform Traps Poor Children." *Education Week* April 27. Accessed April 30, 2011. www.edweek.org/ew/ articles/2011/04/27/29kohn.h30.html.

Kurzweil, Ken. 2010 "Bullied: A Student, a School and a Case That Made History." New York State United Teachers: *NYSUT United*. December 2010.

Lickona, Thomas and Matthew Davidson. n.d. "School as a Caring Community Profile-II (SCCP-II)." The Center for the 4th and 5th Rs: Respect and Responsibility at SUNY Cortland. Accessed April 7, 2011. www2.cortland.edu/ centers/character/.

Little, L. 2002. "Middle-Class Mothers' Perceptions of Peer and Sibling Victimization Among Children with Asperger's Syndrome and Nonverbal Learning Disorders." *Issues in Comprehensive Pediatric Nursing*. 2002 Jan-Mar; 25(1):43–57. www. ncbi.nlm.nih.gov/pubmed/11934121.

"Managing Escalating Behavior." n.d. Center for Positive Behavioral Prevention and Support US Department of Education Office of Special Education Programs. Accessed June 22, 2011. ed.sc.gov/.

McEvoy, Alan. 2005. "Teachers Who Bully Students: Patterns and Policy." Accessed June 22, 2011. Implicationscivilitypartners.com/yahoo_site_admin/assets/docs/teachers_who_bully_students.239164537.pd.

Mendler, Allen.1992. *What Do I Do When? How to Achieve Discipline with Dignity in the Classroom.* Indiana: National Educational Service.

Neiman, Samantha. 2011. "Crime, Violence, Discipline, and Safety in U.S. Public Schools: Findings From the School Survey on Crime and Safety: 2009–10." U.S. Department of Education, National Center for Education Statistics. Accessed March 31, 2011. nces.ed.gov/ pubs2011/2011320.pd.

Ollove, Michael. 2010. "Bullying and Teen Suicide: How Do We Adjust School Climate?" *Christian Science Monitor.* Accessed April 28, 2011. www.csmonitor.com.

Paley, Vivian Gussey. 1992. *You Can't Say You Can't Play.* Cambridge, Massachusetts: Harvard University Press.

Perkins, H. Wesley and David W. Craig. n.d. "The Social Norms Approach." *Your Health and Safety.* Accessed June 5, 2011. youthhealthsafety.hws.edu.

Perkins, H. Wesley and Jessica M. Perkins, David W. Craig. 2009. "Misperceptions of Bullying Norms as a Risk Factor Associated with Violence Among Middle School Students" November 7–11. Accessed June 21, 2011. www.youthhealthsafety.org/MispercepBullyNormsAPHA09 Handouts.pd.

Potok, Mark. 2010. "Anti-Gay Hate Crimes: Doing the Math." *Intelligence Report.* Southern Poverty Law Center. Winter 2010 Issue 140.

Project SAVE. 2000. Schools Against Violence in Education. New York State Center for School Safety. Accessed March 15, 2011. nyscenterforschoolsafety .org/savesummary.pdf.

Robers, S., Zhang, J., and Truman, J. (2010). "Indicators of School Crime and Safety: 2010" (NCES 2011–002/NCJ 230812). National Center for Education Statistics, U.S. Department of Education, and Bureau of Justice Statistics, Office of Justice Programs, U.S. Department of Justice. Washington, DC. Accessed June 6, 2011. nces.ed.gov/pubs2011/2011002.pdf.

Rose, Lowell C. and Alec M. Gallup. 2000. "32nd Annual Phi Delta Kappa/Gallup Poll of the Public's Attitudes Toward Public Schools." Accessed June 18, 2011. moralissues.web.fc2.com/mi/ kpollv82.pdf.

Rose, Lowell C. and Alec M. Gallup. 2007. "39th Annual Phi Delta Kappa/Gallup Poll of the Public's Attitudes Toward Public Schools." Accessed June 16, 2011. www.mikemcmahon.info /PDKpoll2007.pd.

"School Safety Profiler." n.d. Ripple Effects. Accessed May 9, 2011. www .rippleeffects.com/needs/ index.ph.

"School: The Story of American Public Education." 2001. Public Broadcasting System. Accessed May 2, 2011. www.pbs.org/kcet/publicschool/get_involved/guide_p3.html.

Schultz, John and Benita Y. Williams. 2006. "Columbine's Legacy: Haunting, Helpful." *Kansas City Star*. April 22. Accessed April 29, 2011. www.luc.edu/umc/ newsroom/inthenews/042406_8.pdf.

Shindler, John, Jones, Alberta Dee Williams, Clint Taylor, Hermenia Cadenas. 2009. "Exploring Below the Surface: School Climate Assessment and Improvement as the Key to Bridging the Achievement Gap." Accessed June 4, 2011. www .calstatela.edu/faculty/jshindl/cm/ AchievementGapStudyASSC09.htm p.100.

Simmons, Rachel. 2002. *Odd Girl Out: The Hidden Culture of Aggression in Girls*. New York: Harcourt, Inc.

Simons, Rachel. 2011. "What About Boys?" RachelSimmons.com. Accessed June 5, 2011. www.rachelsimmons.com/about-rachel/what-about-boys/.

"Six Steps to Speak Up." n.d. *Teaching Tolerance*. Accessed February 2011. www. tolerance.org/publication/speak/six-steps-speak.

Skiba, Russell J. 2000. "Zero Tolerance, Zero Evidence: An Analysis of School Disciplinary Practice." Policy Report Indiana Education Policy Center Indiana University. August 2000. Accessed June 5, 2011. www.indiana.edu/~safeschl/ztze.pdfp.

"Social Learning: Seven Key Abilities." 1998–2007. Ripple Effects. Accessed May 2, 2011. www.rippleeffects.com/research/background/sociallearning.html.

"Standards of the Heart." n.d. What Are the Characteristics of Successful Schools? n.d. Wisconsin Department of Public Instruction. Accessed April 21, 2011. www .dpi.state.wi.us/cssch/ csssoh1.htm.

Stein, Nan. 2006. "Words Matter: Sweeping Harassment Under the 'Bullying' Rug Does Students a Disservice." *Leadership Insider: Practical Perspectives on School Law and Policy*. National School Boards Association. Accessed March 23, 2011.

Steinberg, Matthew P. and Elaine Allensworth, David W. Johnson. 2011. "Student and Teacher Safety in Chicago Public Schools: The Roles of Community Context and School Social Organization." Consortium on Chicago School Research. Accessed June 24, 2011. ccsr.uchicago.edu/ publications/SAFETY%20IN%20CPS.pd.

Stern-LaRosa, Caryl and Ellen Hohheimer Bettman. 2000. *Hate Hurts: How Children Learn and Unlearn Prejudice*. New York: Scholastic.

"What to Tell Your Child About Prejudice and Discrimination." 2001. Anti-Defamation League. Accessed June 3, 2011. www.adl.org/what_to_tell/whattotell_ learning.asp.

"What is Hazing?" 2011. The National Federation of State High Schools. Accessed June 19, 2011. www.nfhs.org/content.aspx?id=3766.

Young, Jonathan and Ari Ne'eman, Sara Gelser. 2011. "Bullying Students With Disabilities" A Briefing Paper from National Council on Disability. March. Accessed April 6, 2011. www.ncd.gov/publications/2011/March92011.

Young, Sheryl. n.d. "Walk a Mile in their Shoes: Bullying and the Child With Special Needs." AbilityPath.org. Accessed June 28, 2011. www.abilitypath.org/areas-of-development/learning—schools/bullying/articles/walk-a-mile-in-their-shoes.pdf.

"Youth Risk and Behavior Surveillance United States, 2009." 2010. Department of Health and Human Services Centers for Disease Control and Prevention. Accessed March 9, 2011. www.cdc.gov/HealthyYouth/yrbs/index.htm.

About the Author

Elizabeth Cervini Manvell, MS, CAS, has spent her career as a teacher and administrator focusing on the importance of a positive school and classroom climate. She now spends her time thinking, researching, and writing about education. She continues to be inspired by the unique role teachers play in the lives of children and families, and by what compassion and tenacity can accomplish on their behalf. Elizabeth now lives in California with her husband and pets, and is the author of two other books, *Teaching is a Privilege: Twelve Essential Understandings for Beginning Teachers* and *Story Power! Breathing Life Into History.*